MAY 03 '93	DATE DUE	
NOV 8		

CLOSE TO THE CUSTOMER
25 Management Tips from the Other Side of the Counter

JAMES H. DONNELLY, JR.

BUSINESS ONE IRWIN
Homewood, Illinois 60430

Some of the examples in this book have appeared in other formats
and are referenced in James H. Donnelly, Jr. and Steven J.
Skinner, *The New Banker: Developing Leadership in a Dynamic Era*
(Homewood, Ill.: BUSINESS ONE IRWIN, 1989).

© RICHARD D. IRWIN, INC., 1992

This publication is designed to provide accurate and
authoritative information in regard to the subject matter
covered. It is sold with the understanding that neither the
author nor the publisher is engaged in rendering legal, accounting,
or other professional service. If legal advice or other expert
assistance is required, the services of a competent
professional person should be sought.

*From a Declaration of Principles jointly adopted by a Committee
of the American Bar Association and a Committee of Publishers.*

Sponsoring editor:	Jeffrey A. Krames
Project editor:	Gladys True
Production manager:	Bette K. Ittersagen
Interior designer:	Tara L. Bazata
Compositor:	Precision Typographers
Typeface:	11/14 Palatino
Printer:	R. R. Donnelley & Sons Company

Library of Congress Cataloging-in-Publication Data

Donnelly, James H.
   Close to the customer : 25 management tips from the other side of
the counter / James H. Donnelly, Jr.
     p.   cm.
   ISBN 1-55623-569-0
   1. Customer service—Management. 2. Consumer satisfaction.
3. Supervision of employees. 4. Leadership. I. Title.
HF5415.5.D65 1992
658.8'12—dc20   91-3637

Printed in the United States of America

3 4 5 6 7 8 9 0 DOC 8 7 6 5 4 3 2

To 1991 and a year of new beginnings
for a decade of happy endings.

Note

E ach of the encounters I discuss in this book is true. Except where I am the subject of the discussion, names, genders, and circumstances are on occasion fictitious in order to protect the privacy of customers, employees, and organizations. It is not my purpose to embarrass any individual or organization, but rather to teach. No similarity to any specific individual or existing organization is intended, but similarity to all customers, employees, and organizations *is* intended, since that is the point of the book.

Preface

I am a customer and have been for many years. I am very happy to know that we are now being referred to as "King Customer" and that this decade is being forecasted as the "Decade of the Customer" by some of our nation's leading business publications. I've taken this to mean that our time has finally come. So much in fact that I have decided that the world could use a business book based on the experiences and advice of a customer rather than another one based on the experiences and advice of a successful entrepreneur, or chief executive officer.

Customers have much to offer management in three important areas. First, we surely learn a great deal about what it takes to *satisfy customers* since we have the experience of being a customer several times a day. Second, from interacting daily with the employees of a variety of organizations, we also gain a great amount of insight into what seems to work and not work in *managing people*. Finally, from observing the best organizations we deal with and comparing them with the worst, customers cannot help but learn something about *leadership*. Accordingly, these three topics—customer satisfaction, managing people, and leadership—make up the three parts of this book.

The book contains 25 essays. Each one either recounts actual experiences of mine and others in our interactions with the organizations that dominate our lives or it presents a perspective on one of the three topics from the point of view of a customer. More importantly, however, each essay concludes with a lesson for management in either customer satisfaction, managing people, or leadership. I believe these 25 lessons contain important messages for every manager and employee as we enter the Decade of the Customer.

I also believe the reader will find a recurrent theme throughout the book: If the customer is really to be king and this is really the Decade of the Customer, then management must find the relatively few things that matter, and do them very well. In other words, they must do the little things right and the right big things.

I have titled the book *Close to the Customer* because it is likely that you will find some of the essays in the book—particularly those that describe an actual encounter between a customer and an organization—to hit extremely close to home and be painfully familiar. In fact, you have probably had some of the same or very similar encounters and thought the very same thoughts.

The reason for this, of course, is that we are all customers. But most of us also work in organizations that depend on customers, clients, guests, patients, passengers, students, employees, and taxpayers to support the organization. Therefore, it should be relatively easy for an organization to be effective—just do for the customer what we want done when we are the customer. But for some reason it's not that simple. Maybe many of us have two personalities, one which we use when the customer is "us," and another when the customer is "them." And apparently these two people don't have much to say to each other. So this is why I have subtitled the book *25 Management Tips from the Other Side of the Counter*. It is the "customer" in us talking to the "manager" in us.

So, for those who manage or aspire to manage, this book's for you. While I hope you find parts of it humorous, please make no mistake, this is a very serious book. I want to inform, but I also want to inspire you to act because reading and doing nothing will mean we have all wasted our time.

But now it is time to turn the tables. You are now *the customer*. Welcome to my book. I hope I have learned my lessons well.

Jim Donnelly

Contents

PART II   WHAT CUSTOMERS KNOW ABOUT MANAGING PEOPLE

PART III   WHAT CUSTOMERS KNOW ABOUT LEADERSHIP

PART
I

What Customers Know about Customer Satisfaction

One

You Can't Write on the Charmin

"There is only one way under high heaven to get anybody to do anything. And that is by making the other person want to do it."

Dale Carnegie

Businesses are always trying to get customers to change habits and behaviors that they're very comfortable with. For example, I was in a restaurant recently that wanted me to cook my own food. If I wanted to cook, why did I need a restaurant? I've been asked to put a plastic card in a telephone, pay my bills electronically each month, pump my own gas, make my own salad and get my own soup, use a debit card and lose the float I gain when I write a check, and buy fine furniture and then assemble it myself, and last month an airline asked me to carry my own bags out to the plane and put them on a luggage cart parked next

3

to the baggage compartment. I was hoping they wouldn't ask me to serve drinks. Then they lost my bag.

But the very best happened a few years ago. I was new in the area and stopped by a supermarket to stock up the refrigerator in my new apartment. From all appearances, it looked like any other supermarket: lots of merchandise in aisles, check-out registers, and grocery carts.

Was I wrong. Any businesspeople trying to get customers to change their behavior should have been with me that night. They should have charged a cover charge to get in. Not that it was a great supermarket; just a great learning experience.

I grabbed a grocery cart and went about my business, filling it with the items I needed. When I finished I did what we all do at the supermarket when we are ready to leave—I went to the checkout counter. It was there that I learned that I was participating in a real-life experiment in changing customer behavior.

I emptied my cart on the counter and waited for the young woman at the register to begin ringing up the sale. Instead she asked, "Could I please have your crayon, sir?" "Pardon me?" I said. She repeated her request. "Crayon?" I said with a laugh, "I don't have any crayon."

This teenage woman looked at me sternly and said, "Sir, this is a discount supermarket. We have no prices on our merchandise. You were supposed to have picked up a crayon when you entered the store. The prices are shown on the boxes and shelves, and you are supposed to write the price on the product with the black crayon."

"You're kidding me," I said. "No sir, I'm not," she responded. At that point I was going to inform her that I didn't want to play, and leave the store. But she was such a nice person that I gathered up all of my merchandise, put it back into my cart, pushed the cart to where they had a can full of black crayons, and picked one out. I then retraced my entire trip through the store, writing the prices on all of my merchandise. It was at this time that I proved you cannot write on a Charmin wrapper with a black crayon.

I returned to the same check-out counter and was poised and ready when she asked me for my crayon. She checked me through just like in any other supermarket. I was standing there smiling, with my hands in my pockets, when she asked, "Would you like a bag, sir?"

I surveyed my rather large number of items and said, "Bag? Of course I want a bag! How do you think I'm going to get all this stuff home?" Once again she looked at me sternly and said with a little more firmness in her voice, "Sir, this is a discount supermarket; we charge for bags. So some people bring their own."

"Ahah!" I exclaimed, "I should have known, the old bait-and-switch trick. Now that you've got me all checked through, you're going to make me pay to get out. How much are bags, 10 bucks apiece?" "No sir, they are 5 cents each," she replied. "Oh hell, give me three of them," I said.

She laid them neatly on top of my merchandise as I remained standing there. Once again she looked at me, this time with a frustrated look in her eyes and said, "Sir, this is a discount supermarket; we do not bag groceries for you. You have to bag your own groceries."

Now here I was for the first time ever in my life trying to bag groceries. The bananas slipped down next to the Charmin and ripped the side of my first bag. I fumbled through my pockets trying to find another nickel.

As I was bagging my groceries, I began to think of all of my manager friends who say, "Customers won't change! They'll never cook their own food, use the automatic teller, assemble their own furniture, or let us keep their canceled checks at the bank." All I know is that when I was a kid growing up in Brooklyn I told my mother there were two things I would never do to earn spending money. I was never going to be a bagger in a supermarket, and I was never going to pump gas because it was too cold in the winter time. So I took piano lessons so I could work my way through high school and college as a piano player.

Now here I am, middle-aged, and what am I being asked to do? You got it, bag my own groceries and pump my own gas. All these years of school and work and I'm doing something I didn't want to do when I was 15 years old. Where is our country going? If I asked most adults 10 years ago if they had any long-range plans that involved pumping gas, they would have told me I was crazy.

As I finished my third bag of groceries, I also remembered that when I was a kid and visiting my grandmother in southern New Jersey and wanted to call my Aunt Justine I would have to pick up the phone (no dial) and give the operator her number. More than once she would say, "She's not home now; she's down at the beauty parlor. Do you want me to connect you down there?" Last night I made a long-distance credit card phone call that involved remembering 36 numbers. Now that is quite a change from the old days. But I'm glad to do it to avoid ever again having to deal with surly and rude telephone operators.

I also remembered addressing a letter to 102 Center St. Brooklyn, New York. Then they made us memorize a five-digit number, and now in some places they have added four more digits. (Do you think they have a group at the post office who have an office pool to see how many numbers they can get us to memorize by the year 2000?) But we do it because I suppose we are willing to do anything to increase the chances of our mail arriving at its destination in a reasonable amount of time.

The point of course is that customers do change their behavior. But they do it when *they* want to do it, *not* when management wants them to do it.

We are pumping our own gas, cooking our own food in some restaurants, memorizing between 30 and 40 numbers to make a long-distance call, using the zip code system, and helping commuter airlines handle baggage (so they don't have an opportunity to lose it and so we don't have to wait in the terminal). We are doing these things because we

---

You must often try to convince customers to change habits and behaviors that they are very comfortable with and to do things they didn't want to do when they were 15 years old.

---

want to. There is some incentive that we apparently feel is worth changing our behavior for.

We are not smoking smokeless cigarettes and not using the debit card, and apparently we like to see our canceled checks at the end of every month rather than let the bank keep them. We are not doing these things even though the cigarette manufacturer and the banking industry would like us to. No matter how much money they spend trying to convince us, we do not change our behavior. We are not doing these things because there is at this time apparently no incentive worth changing our behavior for. We don't want to. It's that simple.

Incidentally, if you're wondering whatever happened to the discount supermarket, it didn't make it. Apparently, the incentive of lower prices was not enough to get sufficient numbers of customers to write the prices on their merchandise, pay for bags, and bag their own groceries. Thank goodness.

Lesson #1

There Are Only Two Conditions under Which Customers Will Change Their Behavior:
1. When It's a Matter of Life and Death (and Then Not in Every Case).
2. If They Want to—If They Are Given a Reason to Change.

Two
You Can Care Enough to Send Some Soap

"A person who looks inward is bound to try to make the times try to fit his company's products."

Peter C. Vink

W hen my mother was 72 years old, I decided to do something special for her. After about a week of thinking about it, I realized that 72 divided by 12 was 6. My idea was to send my mother 72 roses (6 dozen) for her 72nd birthday. Since her birthday was on May 5th, I would send two dozen yellow roses on May 4th, two dozen red roses on May 5th, and two dozen peach roses on May 6th. And I would have the "Son of the Year Award" locked up.

On May 4th when she got the first dozen, she called and I was "Son of the Year." (Of course on May 6th she called and said, "The living room looks like a funeral parlor.") But on the afternoon of May 4th, I realized I had forgotten something. Anyone can send 72 roses. All you have to do is call a florist and say "I want two dozen yellow on May 4th, two dozen red on May 5th, and two dozen peach on May 6th, and make each one in a different arrangement."

I had forgotten the one thing that costs the least but takes the most time. You have to go to a store and buy it, address it, find a stamp for it, and mail it. I had spent $296.00 for roses and was about to blow "Son of the Year" for a lousy $1.25 birthday card. I headed immediately for a card shop.

Now I'm not sure, but since I don't spend a great deal of time in card shops, this visit may have been my first ever to a local card shop. All I knew is that I needed a birthday card and my mother was going to become the first woman in America to receive a birthday card via Federal Express.

On that day if you asked me, "What business is Hallmark (or a similar business) in?" I would have said, "Greeting cards," which I suspect is what many people would have said. I couldn't have been further off the mark, as I was about to find out.

I purchased my mother's birthday card at the card shop and was waiting in line to pay for it. For some reason I noticed several small packages on the counter that contained about 12 small round pieces of soap. They were all different colors, smelled great, and were attractively wrapped in a basketlike package.

I thought to myself, "If I were to buy one of these and send it to an important woman in my life as a surprise, a few days later I would get a phone call from a happy person.'' She would thank me and probably tell me what a thoughtful, kind, considerate, and generous man I am. I would have done a good thing.

But as I paid for the birthday card, I thought to myself, "Suppose I sent that very same woman 12 bars of Zest?" I almost certainly would have never received a phone call from her (which is probably what I would have been hoping to accomplish by sending the Zest in the first place). If she did call, however, I'm sure she would have told me (among other things) that I was a thoughtless, unkind, cruel, and insensitive man.

Now wait a minute, unless women use those little bars of soap for something I don't know anything about, soap is soap. If you mail someone some soap, aren't you saying, "Hey, take a bath!" It began to puzzle me greatly. How can I send Hallmark soap and be thoughtful and considerate, and send Procter & Gamble soap and be insensitive and cruel? Even if I purchased my own basket, ribbon, and cellophane wrap, and unwrapped each bar of Zest, individually wrapped each one with cellophane and ribbon, and then wrapped the entire basket, it still wouldn't make a difference. All the extra expense and effort wouldn't count for anything. I would still be a cruel and hurtful man. I would have done a bad thing.

Why was this situation such a puzzle to me? Because I made the same mistake many managers make. I was defining the business in terms of a product (greeting cards) rather than in terms of the needs customers satisfy by using the business. I was like a thoroughbred racehorse running down the stretch with blinders on. My vision was

very narrow, my sense of possibilities very limited. Hallmark does not make the mistake I made. They do not have
blinders on. They don't think of their business as only
greeting cards, as I did. They know that Americans have a
great need to relate and we can relate to each other in many
other ways than just greeting cards.

The next time I walked into a Hallmark store I took my
blinders off. And I saw greeting cards, buttons, stuffed animals, T-shirts, ribbons, books of poems, relationship cards,
figurines, wall hangings, wrapping paper, and cards for

---

*Never define your business in terms of its current
products. You will be like a thoroughbred racehorse
running down the stretch with blinders on. Your
vision is very narrow, your sense of possibilities very
limited.*

---

secretaries day, mothers-in-law, cats, and sweetest day. I
saw humorous cards, postcards, cards with no verse, and
balloons. And yes, I saw soap.

Now I understand. Hallmark knows that our needs to
relate to each other are a broad class, not a narrow individual need that can be satisfied only through greeting
cards. They understand what their business is and so do
we. That is why whenever we get something from someone that says Hallmark on it we feel warm fuzzies. Even if
it happens to be soap, because we know that Hallmark is

"When you care enough to send the very best." Hallmark understands that our needs usually come in clusters and they organize themselves internally to satisfy these broad classes of needs.

Do you remember in the old days when the healthcare industry was organized by functional specialties (individual practitioners)? It was organized for the convenience of the medical practitioner, not for the convenience of the customer. Do you recall the process? If there was something wrong with you, you visited the family doctor who said, "You have something wrong with you. I'll make an appointment for you to get an X ray next week downtown." After the X ray you went back to your doctor, and he said, "Yup, just what I thought. We need to make an appointment with a specialist." So the next week you went to the other side of town to the specialist. And of course, by the time you saw the specialist and got all the reports, you were dead.

The revolution in healthcare delivery was a result of the recognition that, just like our relationship needs, our healthcare needs do not come in individual bits and pieces. They come in bunches, clusters, or broad classes. In other words, if you have a need for diagnosis, chances are you have need for other medical services as well. The clinic concept, HMO concept, and sports medicine centers reflect the recognition by the healthcare industry that our healthcare needs come in clusters. The industry has figured out ways to organize internally to satisfy these needs.

Hallmark and the healthcare industry are not the only examples. The travel agency saves us the trouble of having to deal with four or five separate organizations to satisfy all of our needs to put together a vacation. The modern church recognizes that we have more spiritual needs than just to worship on Sunday and organizes itself to satisfy our cluster of spiritual needs.

The point is a very important one: As customers, we rarely have *a need*, we usually have *needs*.

Lesson #2

Our Needs Usually Come in Clusters, Not in Bits and Pieces. The Best Organizations Organize Themselves to Satisfy Clusters of Customer Needs.

Three

Never Keep a Secret

"Policy-making is not as easy as slurping down cabbage soup. . . . As the saying goes, before going into the room, make sure you can get out."

Yegor Ligachev

A while back, I needed 1,000 25 cent stamps for a project I was working on. I discussed the operational details with the people who were assisting me, and we decided that rolls of stamps would be far more efficient than sheets of stamps for 1,000 pieces of mail that had to be stamped in a short period of time.

When I arrived at the post office, I found several available windows. All were closed but one (for a moment I thought I was in a bank). There was one window open, but no one was working at it. As I stood there, I noticed several people sitting at their desks doing post office kinds of things. Occasionally someone would look up at me but immediately drop their eyes back to their desk. One man had his arms folded and was face down in them.

After a while a man walked past the window and glanced at me. In a few minutes he walked back past the window with a cup in his hand, but didn't look at me. Finally, thinking that I might have become invisible, I yelled, "Customer! Customer!"

A young man finally came up to the window. Knowing that 25 cent stamps come in rolls of 100, I said, "Could I please have 10 rolls of 25 cent stamps?" I put $250 on the counter and asked for a receipt.

He looked in his drawer for a moment and said, "I can give you sheets." I told him that I did not want or need sheets because they would be inefficient for my purpose. I needed 10 rolls of 25 cent stamps.

He looked in his drawer again and said, "If I sell you 10 rolls of 25 cent stamps, I won't have any left in my drawer." Naively, I said, "Great! You're having a good day. You've sold out."

"No," he replied. I was wrong. If he sold me 10 rolls of 25 cent stamps, he wouldn't have any rolls left for other customers who come to his window during his shift. There was nothing he could do because it was policy.

Shocked, I said, "But you don't understand how business works. The idea is to sell out. That's good!" Fumbling for words I said, "Suppose I went to a men's clothing store and said to the owner, 'I really love your selection of 41-long sport jackets. In fact, I love them so much, I'll take them all.' He would not say 'I'm sorry sir, I can't do that because next Thursday someone might come in looking for a 41-long sport jacket and I won't have one.' " As nicely as I could I explained that every businessperson I knew had a recurring fantasy of selling out.

When that didn't work, I suggested an alternative. I would purchase four rolls now. I would return later (perhaps in disguise if necessary), purchase three more, and so on.

As I climbed into my car with 1,000 stamps in sheets, I realized that I had just learned an important lesson about customer satisfaction, which unfortunately for me would be repeated a short time later in Chicago.

I was browsing in the fabulous Water Tower Place, a collection of some of the finest stores in the world. I spotted a sweater in the window of a department store that I wanted very much. Unfortunately, I was informed by a salesperson that the store was out of stock in all sizes and would not be getting any more in. Disappointed, I left the store.

As I walked past the window display and took one more glance at the sweater I wanted so much, I was delighted to see that it was my size. Excited, I returned to the store and found the same salesperson.

"It might be a bit hard to reach," I said, "but the one in the window is my size." "Oh sir," the salesperson informed me, "we *never* take anything out of the window." "Never?" I asked. "Do you mean that sweater is going to be in the window for the rest of my life?" She informed me that it was company policy not to take anything out of the window.

I pleaded that since there were none in stock in any size and no additional stock was coming in all this policy could possibly result in was one lost sale and more disappointed customers like me. And she could avoid all of these problems by selling me the sweater. I've had to learn to live without the sweater.

The above incidents illustrate some important points. First, if customers' satisfaction is subject to certain conditions, they would like to know what they are before they arise. Second, more often than not, policies like those above make absolutely no sense to the customer. They are inexplicable to a sane person. Third, if the truth were known, such secret policies probably do not exist in most cases. They seem to be invented on the spot by employees for their own convenience in order to avoid additional work. They are the employee's secret.

For example, I really doubt whether the post office has a policy that prevents employees from selling out. However, selling out probably creates additional work for the employee. In his case it probably would mean counting out

---

Never inconvenience a customer for the sake of the organization or an employee.

---

some cash, locking the drawer, going to a central place to purchase additional rolls of stamps, maybe filling out a form or two, and returning to the window.

Also, in a recent identical situation in a department store, the salesperson informed me that she could not take an item out of a window display. However, she went the extra step and put forth the effort to take my name, address, and credit card information and promised to mail me the item when it was removed from the window. She did not hide behind a secret policy.

In any case, I have to be one of the few people who can only get sheets at a post office and can't get a sweater at a department store.

Lesson #3

Customers Should Never Be Inconvenienced Because of Company Policies that Are Known Only to Employees—and Do Not Become Known to Customers Until They Are Used Against Them.

Four

Hand-Offs Only Work in Football

"If you ever live in a country run by a committee, be on the committee."

Lao Tzu

For most of us who have had a basic course in economics, we understand at least one principle of pricing. If we buy 10 pounds of sugar, we can expect to pay more than for 5 pounds of sugar. Now the price per pound may be less since we are buying a larger quantity, but the total price for 10 pounds will be greater than the total price for 5 pounds. We know and we accept this. It is fair.

However, if someone tried to charge us more for a two-pound box of sugar than for a five-pound box of sugar (assuming they were of the same quality), we would certainly balk—especially if we only wanted two pounds of sugar.

We would ask, "Why should I spend more to get less? This supermarket either thinks I'm stupid or knows nothing about how to set prices."

At this point you are probably thinking, "No business-person would ever do such a thing." Well, you are wrong. And while this essay is not about how to set prices, the problem and lesson are the outcome of a customer being asked to spend more and get less.

It all began on the second evening of a 13-night stay in a hotel in the Northwest. Most hotel managers would surely agree that someone staying 13 nights in a hotel represents a pretty good customer. The average stay in a hotel is probably a great deal less than 13 nights. The room charges, meals, cocktails, and so on for 13 nights no doubt add up to a considerable sum of money.

On my second morning in the hotel, I reached for the shampoo while in the shower and couldn't find any. I climbed out of the shower and called the front desk and said, "This is Donnelly in Room 918, could you please send up some shampoo." The front-desk clerk replied, "When did you check in, Mr. Donnelly?" "What difference does it make?" I inquired.

The desk clerk informed me that it was a policy of the hotel to provide guests shampoo only on their first night and I had just completed my second night. "Wait a minute!" I said. "I'm staying 13 nights in this hotel. Do you mean to tell me that you do more for a customer who stays 1 night than for someone who stays 13 nights?" I asked him if the first-night-only policy also applied to sheets, towels, and pillowcases. Fortunately the answer was *no*. "So then why does it apply to shampoo?" I asked. He said I would have to ask the front-desk manager and put me on hold.

I was getting frustrated when the front-desk manager finally picked up the phone. I decided I was acting on principle (I had plenty of my own shampoo in my shaving kit). Besides, my curiosity had gotten the best of me. I wanted to find out the rationale for such a policy—if one even existed.

I commented to the front-desk manager that I had never heard of a business that does less for a customer the more they spend. It seemed logical that a person staying 13 nights should get shampoo every night and a customer staying only 1 night shouldn't get any. I tried to illustrate to him that down at the bank the longer you leave your money in the

Playing "stump-the-customer" should be a TV game show. Although I was staying 13 nights, the hotel's policy was shampoo on the first night only. I asked if the same first-night-only policy applied to sheets, towels, and pillowcases.

more interest they pay you. I pointed out that if this hotel were a bank they would be paying higher interest rates if I left my money in the bank for a shorter length of time. Those people who left their money in the bank for longer periods of time would get lower rates of interest. He said he didn't work at the bank and I needed to talk to the general manager of the hotel, and then he put me on hold again.

By the time the general manager picked up his phone, my patience had run out. I promised him I would go away if he would just explain the rationale for the policy. I said I had never heard of a business that does less for a customer the more they spend and that the policy only made sense if the hotel was trying to promote one-night stands instead of thirteen-night stands. This suggestion seemed to irritate the general manager greatly.

Any chance of getting an explanation of the policy or my shampoo now appeared slim. It became zero when I noted that the hotel appeared to me to be only 50 percent occupied, and I suggested to the general manager my solution to the problem. I would check out every morning and check back in every night for the remaining 11 nights. I told him I would be checking out in a little while and asked whether he could make me a reservation for that evening. Thus I would be eligible to have some shampoo every morning, which was consistent with hotel policy. For some reason he suggested I find another hotel.

Stop for a moment and recall the previous essay, "Never Keep a Secret." This incredible hotel encounter presents another great example of Lesson #3.

First, no one informed me of the policy when I checked into the hotel. The desk clerk did not say, "Hey buddy, you better have some shampoo for the day after tomorrow because you sure as hell aren't going to get any here."

Second, the policy makes absolutely no sense to a sane person (unless, as I suggested, the hotel was trying to encourage one-night stands). Furthermore, no one was able to explain the rationale for the policy to a customer who was staying 13 nights.

Finally, I did not become aware of the policy until it was used against me—I was standing dripping wet and naked in the middle of my hotel room when I first heard about it.

In this particular instance the customer's problem was never resolved (I was invited to leave the hotel). But be that as it may (my attitude may have been partially to blame), I believe I learned another important lesson in this hotel as I was passed on from the front-desk clerk to the front-desk manager and finally to the general manager.

In any business, a customer's problem should be resolved at the point at which it arises. If management is familiar enough with the business they are in, then they should be familiar with (1) what customer problems are most likely to arise and (2) where they are most likely to arise. Then the employees at those points should be empowered to solve these problems within specified limits. The entire incident at the hotel occurred because the desk clerk was not empowered to solve a guest's problem with a one-ounce bottle of shampoo.

Lesson #4

Customers Should Never Be Required to Restate Their Request or Complaint to Several Employees Before Having It Resolved.

Five

We May Not Get What We Deserve, but We Always Get What We Expect

"What you stroke is what you get."

Eric Berne

Not too long ago I was to have dinner with someone in one of the finest restaurants in town. It was to be an early dinner and we arrived just after 5 o'clock. The restaurant was empty, so we got a nice table by a window.

We were the only customers during our entire meal and got plenty of attention from our waitress. She was a pleasant, talkative, and naive young woman. We struck up an immediate friendship with her and chatted throughout our entire meal.

Another couple came in as we were finishing our meal. The host seated the couple at a table next to ours. I could not help but overhear what they ordered. One thing they ordered with their meal was a Caesar salad. The waitress went back to the kitchen and rolled the salad cart toward their table. However, rather than stop at their table she rolled the cart to our table. I assume it was because she wanted to continue chatting with us as she prepared their salad.

"This is the first Caesar salad I've ever made in my life," she said. With that I saw the man at the next table start to squirm a little and glance over at our table. "In fact," she said, "I had never even heard of one before I started working here."

I tried my best to send mental signals to this nice young woman that she should not pursue this conversation. Here they were in one of the finest restaurants in town, paying premium prices for the food, and the couple is listening to an employee inform everyone that she had never before prepared what they were about to eat. My attempt at mental telepathy failed.

"But I watched my manager make one last week and snuck a leaf out of the bowl to taste it while the customers weren't looking," she said. "I didn't particularly like it."

Now there was some squirming at our table as I had visions of her sticking her finger in my cream of mushroom soup while she was bringing it from the kitchen. I prayed that everything we had ordered she had tasted at some time earlier in her life. Then I remembered that the corner of my filet of sole almandine was missing.

She delivered the salads professionally and returned to the kitchen with the cart. I made a silent prediction to myself, which came true in less than a minute. I heard the woman at the next table say, "This is the worst Caesar salad I've ever had in my life." Although we didn't stay around to witness the remainder of their dinner, I have a strong feeling her opinion didn't change much.

The friendly, well-intentioned employee had, unknown to herself or her manager, taught me something about customers and customer expectations that would be reinforced on two different occasions after that night.

The first occasion was when I happened to be flying my least favorite airline. Now don't ask me why I have a favorite and a least favorite airline. They all fly the same planes and go to the same cities. It must have something to do with the people who work for and manage these businesses.

I was sitting in an aisle seat when a tiny woman in her seventies or eighties stopped at my row and told me that her seat was by the window. She opened the storage compartment above the seat to store a bag when the luggage already there began to slide out. This elderly woman was bent over backwards trying to keep the luggage from falling on top of her when I jumped out of my seat, pushed the luggage back into the compartment, and helped the woman into her seat. All the while I watched three flight attendants chatting in the plane's galley, in full view of the woman. They ignored the entire incident. Somehow I know (expect) that the flight attendants on my favorite airline would have been there to help this elderly woman.

Later in the flight the attendants were passing out snacks when they ran out—just as they got to me. I told the attendant that I understood and that I really didn't want one anyway as I was going to dinner as soon as we arrived. The attendant apologized. Then she added with a smile, "What do you expect from this airline?"

When we landed a short time later, I went to the baggage claim area to pick up my luggage. My bags had not made the connecting flight. I went to the desk and was told that they would come in on the first flight the next morning. As I walked out of the airport, I remembered saying the very same thing that the flight attendant had said, "What do you expect from this airline?"

The second incident occurred after a grueling five-day trip in which I had been in three cities. When the plane landed I was exhausted and almost fell asleep during the short cab ride home.

Though I was tired, I was also very hungry. I wanted some fresh seafood. Because I had been gone for a week, my cupboard was bare. I dragged myself out to my car and drove some distance to a food market.

It was the first time I had been in the store and I was impressed. I really liked their seafood counter. It was clean, and stocked with fresh varieties of just about any kind of seafood a customer would want.

I spent a few minutes window-shopping and then spotted the orange roughy, which happens to be one of my favorite kinds of fish. It was fresh and very attractive. I decided my dinner would be some sautéed orange roughy with peas and mushrooms.

I ordered a pound of orange roughy from the man behind the counter. As he was weighing and wrapping it, I was praising his fish counter. "I have never seen a bigger variety of fresh fish in this town," I said. "This is really something, and I now know where to come to get fresh fish. I'm really excited about this because I love seafood."

He finished wrapping my orange roughy, and as he handed it to me over the counter he said, "If you worked here as long as I have, there's a lot of this stuff you'd never eat again for the rest of your life."

As I walked to my car I thought, "I hope he wasn't referring to my orange roughy." That night I ate all of my peas and mushrooms but didn't finish all of the orange roughy, and I haven't been back to that fresh seafood counter again.

Many psychologists believe that expectations are a key to understanding human behavior. I doubt that anyone would argue that the extent of our satisfaction with a product, service, employee, business, relationship, or anything for that matter is greatly determined by our expectations. Very simply, if our expectations are met or exceeded, we are satisfied. If they are not met, we are not satisfied. It matters little if our expectations are unrealistic or not.

When dealing with customer expectations, it is always better to ''underpromise and overperform'' than to ''overpromise and underperform.''

For example, one hotel had to stop their promise of a free night if anything went wrong because they could not live up to the expectations they had set. Another hotel is sorry they ever promised a free breakfast if room service were not on time, and several banks are wondering why they ever promised cash for every mistake they made.

It is easy to see that setting expectations too high can cause customer dissatisfaction if the company cannot deliver. But as we have seen here, the opposite is even more explosive. Every day employees unwittingly establish negative expectations as the above incidents illustrate. And once established, negative expectations are very easy to satisfy.

Lesson #5

*If You Establish Negative
Expectations for Your Customers,
You Will Always Meet Them.*

Six

Sometimes Service Means Having to Say You're Sorry

"Do not put a sword into a madman's hand."

English Proverb

F or those who travel a great deal, I'm sure the following account of one day on the road will have some familiar rings.

My flight was due around 10 P.M. but was delayed in Atlanta because of bad weather. I guess I arrived around midnight. I was quite surprised to find that the limo driver was standing at the appropriate place holding a card with my name on it. I had assumed he would have left hours ago and was very happy to see him.

He grabbed my bags and we climbed into his van and headed for a hotel on the Gulf Coast, some 40 or 50 miles from the airport. "I know you have to get up early Mr. Donnelly," he said, "so I'll do my best to get you to the hotel as fast as I can." I was very tired and was glad to hear what he said.

In a short time we were about 10 or 15 miles out of town, somewhere on a dark two-lane road between there and the coast. I wasn't paying attention to how fast we were going, but I was bouncing around the van quite a bit when I heard the siren and saw the flashing lights.

When the trooper approached the van, it was obvious that he was upset. He informed the driver that he had been going far over the speed limit and asked him to step out of the van. I tried to appear invisible in the backseat.

But I began to become a little concerned when the driver inquired of the trooper, "Why aren't you out trying to catch some criminals instead of bothering a working guy who is trying to make a living?" He then brought me into the argument by saying that my plane was late and all he was trying to do was to get me to bed as soon as possible because I had to be up very early in the morning.

I could hear the argument escalating outside the van, and it became obvious to me that the trooper was about to arrest the driver. Fear began to grip me. What am I going to do? I have no idea where I am and have never driven a van. What is a little New York boy like me going to do somewhere in the middle of the swamps? All of a sudden I had visions of the cast from *Deliverance* showing up with their pointy ears and their banjos.

With that I climbed out of the van and intervened. I convinced the trooper that my driver was a well-intentioned young man who was just trying to help a distressed traveler. When everyone calmed down, the trooper wrote a ticket for the driver and we were back on our way. Feeling partially responsible for the driver's plight, I gave him $75, which he said would be enough to cover the cost of the ticket.

I guess it was sometime after 2 A.M. when we arrived at the hotel. Exhausted, I went to bed.

I was up at 6 A.M. to attend my meeting. Since I was checking out at noon to return home, I came back to my room at the 10 A.M. meeting break to pack. I returned to my room about noon to pick up my bags and go downstairs to the desk to check out. It was then that I noticed that the message light was flashing on the telephone.

When the operator had finished giving me my message, I asked if she knew what time the message came in. She replied, "Eight P.M. last evening." Fortunately, the message was not, "You have three hours to claim your $1 million Sweepstakes prize." But as I went down to the front desk to check out, I remember being a little concerned that I had not received the message when I checked in, which was what the caller had requested.

While at the front desk checking out, I noticed a woman walk past with a name tag that read "Front Desk Manager." I did not intend to complain but rather to inform her what had happened. I motioned her over to me, introduced myself, and told her my story.

She did not apologize on behalf of the hotel. Instead she said, "I do not answer the phones, sir." Stunned for a moment, I replied, "Neither do I, so I guess that makes us even."

"What time did you check in?" she asked. "Sometime around 2 A.M.," I replied. "Well, that explains it," she said. "The people whose job it is to do that leave at about 11 P.M."

When I told her that my message light was not on when I awoke around 6 A.M., she said, "Well, those people don't come to work until around 8 A.M."

When I told her that I returned to my room at 10 A.M. to pack and the light was not on, she said, "You probably didn't see it. Sometimes they are difficult to see during the day."

With that comment I began to recount the last 12 hours of my life: the exciting van ride, the state trooper, the altercation, the $75 the ride cost me, and to top it all, this absurd game I was playing with the front-desk manager.

I slammed my hand on the counter and said, "Look miss, I am checking out of this hotel and if I get really lucky, I will never be back. I am not looking for a complimentary meal or a box of candy, as I am on my way to the airport. I did not tell you this to complain. I saw you walk

---

Managers are supposed to solve problems. If a manager is not interested in identifying problems, then there is no reason for the manager.

---

by, saw you were the front-desk manager, and thought you would, or at least should, want to know what happened. But after our conversation I can readily understand why I did not get my message."

With that grand finale, I walked out of the hotel. As I rode to the airport, I wondered why the entire ridiculous encounter had to occur in the first place. A simple acknowledgement or apology would have ended the problem on a happy note. I would have felt that I had done the hotel a service by informing them of the mishap, and their acknowledgement would have made me happy, and a win-win situation would have resulted.

But the behavior of the employee turned the situation into a lose-lose one. Undoubtedly fresh out of an assertiveness training course, the front-desk manager did her best to turn the situation around to where I was explaining my behavior for a problem the hotel caused. She was determined not to accept personal responsibility for my problem and did her best to absolve the hotel of any responsibility. An employee will always lose such contests of mental gymnastics with a customer. And even if the employee should win, the organization will always lose.

Lesson #6

Quality Service Means Never Having to Say, ''That's Not My Job.''

Seven

It's Not Our Job

"Don't fight a battle if you don't gain anything by winning."
General George S. Patton, Jr.

One of the advantages of flying west is that you always pick up a few hours and are able to arrive at a comfortable time. And so it was that after a lengthy plane trip I arrived at my hotel in Arizona at 1 P.M.

And what a hotel it was. Apparently it was a golf resort, and everything about it was plush or bordering on the ostentatious. It took up so much land that guests had to be driven to their rooms in golf carts.

Since I did not have to be at my meeting until 6 P.M., I was looking forward to getting settled in my room and taking a

49

long walk around the hotel grounds on this beautiful Arizona afternoon. Unfortunately, it was not to be.

When I went to the front desk to register, a young woman informed me that my room was not ready. "Come back in about 15 minutes," she said. I remember thinking that it would be quite a trick for me to see her in 15 minutes since I had waited 25 minutes in line the first time.

I guess I sat in the lobby of the hotel for over 30 minutes before I went back and stood in line. When I finally made it to the counter, she once again informed me that my room was not ready and that this time maybe I should come back in 30 minutes.

I checked my luggage with the bellman and decided I would give the woman an hour before I returned. It was now after 2 P.M., but I was not yet concerned since my meeting was not until 6 P.M. I strolled the grounds, got something to eat, and returned at 3:15. I was now on a first-name basis with the desk clerk since we had already spent so much time together, and we were starting to develop a relationship.

The relationship began to sour a little when she told me that my room was still not ready. I said, "Maria, give me a broom. I can clean a room in 15 minutes, and I've been here since 1 o'clock." I told her I had a meeting at 6 P.M. that I needed to be dressed for. She assured me that it would be no longer than 15 minutes. I found a plush chair in the overly ostentatious lobby to continue my wait.

It was 4:45 when I woke up in a panic. I ran to the counter to find Maria and my room key. "I'm sorry Mr. Donnelly," she said, "but we still do not have a room ready for you."

At this point I became self-righteous (and loud). I demanded a room on every legal and moral ground I could think of. "OK!" Maria snapped, "if you do not want to wait for your room, I will find another one for you."

As the bellman drove me to my room in a golf cart, I had no idea what Maria really meant by finding another room for me. The first thing I noticed was that I could see grass and earth from my high windows. Yes, my room was basically underground. I had to look up to see the ground. Happy to be in a room, I tipped the bellman and sent him on his way. Maria had gotten even.

As the bellman drove away, I realized that he had left my attache case at the bellman's stand. Rather than call and wait for them to drive it to my room, I decided I could walk to the lobby and back quicker.

When I returned to my room, I found that someone had already stacked my underwear on the bed. "Wow!" I thought, "I've been in a lot of nice hotels, but I've never experienced a housekeeping service like this one." I was right. On closer inspection I realized the underwear was not mine. When I opened the closet door, I found a collection of four or five very attractive shirts. Unfortunately they were also not mine. They had the name Tommy Wong attached to them from the hotel's dry cleaner. I figured it was time to call my friend Maria.

For some reason Maria seemed to have trouble remembering who I was. When I finally jogged her memory, she apologized on behalf of the hotel and said that they had obviously delivered the laundry and dry cleaning to the wrong room. She would send a bellman up shortly to pick up the clothing. Fortunately, he showed up in a few minutes.

Relieved, I prepared to take a shower and get ready for my 6 P.M. meeting, which was coming up shortly. This hotel was so upscale that the room had a separate shower stall. I was looking forward to a shower as I opened the door. Inside, I saw two bottles of half-used extra-strength shampoo. Each one was for chronic dandruff, scaling scalps, and psoriasis of the head and scalp. One bottle's contents looked like kerosene. I quickly slammed the door and went to call Maria.

I told Maria several things. First, that hotel security should check the grounds to ensure that Tommy Wong was

---

Never insult a customer's intelligence or expectations. Only the valedictorian of an assertiveness training school would try to convince a hotel guest who had missed a meeting because he had to wait five hours for a room that it was unreasonable for him to expect a room to be ready in a hotel whose business it is to have rooms ready.

---

not lying at the bottom of the swimming pool. Second, that they should check the grounds for an Asian man wearing no underwear and scratching his head feverishly. Third, I asked her if perhaps I was using the room in the daytime and Tommy Wong got to use it at night. She did not appreciate my humor. Finally, I told her that I would not stay in the room I had been assigned to under any circumstances. I packed up and went back to the front desk to confront Maria.

It was now past 6 P.M. I had been in the hotel since 1 P.M. I was late for my meeting, so I fully expected some TLC from Maria and the hotel when I arrived back at the front desk.

Instead Maria was very upset. In a loud and very stern voice she said, "Mr. Donnelly, if you had not forced me to put you in this room and instead had waited for the room I was going to assign to you, none of this would have happened and you would now be at your meeting!"

After waiting for a room in the hotel for five hours, it was now my fault that I had missed my meeting. I asked Maria if she had attended the same assertiveness training course as the front-desk manager in the previous essay.

Recall that in that incident I was told, "That's not my job," when I informed the front-desk manager that I had received a telephone message 18 hours after it arrived. But what I liked best about her was that not only did she tell me it was not her job, she tried to tell me it was *my job*. Recall also that according to her I didn't get my message because I got in too late, got up too early, and couldn't see very well in the daytime.

Now Maria was trying to do the same thing to me. It was my fault that I missed my meeting because I had expected a room to be ready in a hotel whose business it is to have rooms ready. It was not their problem that I arrived in Phoenix at 1 P.M. If I had arrived at 5:30, my room would have been ready and I would not have had to wait. I was the cause of the problem. I did not fall for this trick in the Gulf Coast hotel and was not about to do so in Arizona.

Why must some organizations behave as if the customer is an enemy? As in the Gulf Coast hotel, a simple acknowledgement that a problem or mistake had occurred and a simple apology would have ended the situation on a happy note. It is bad enough for a customer to hear, ''That's not my job.'' But it is an even bigger crime when the customer is also told, ''It is your job,'' or when the customer is blamed because an employee or the organization refuses to accept responsibility for a mistake or a problem.

Lesson #7

The Delivery of Quality Service Is Never the Customer's Job.

Eight

The Best Can Be
the Worst

"Before you build a better mousetrap, it helps to know if there are any mice out there."

Mortimer B. Zuckerman

Ever since I can remember, I have traveled with a small wind-up alarm clock. I received it as a gift many years ago. It has always been a dependable travel companion and has always sounded its alarm when I asked it to.

But there has always been one thing I didn't like about it. It has a very loud tick. If there is one thing that can keep me awake, it is the ticking of a clock next to my ear. I have always solved the problem by placing the clock under the bed in my hotel room.

I have found out, however, that the solution to the ticking problem has caused some additional problems. First,

57

because the clock is under the bed, a sound sleep or a humming air conditioner can cause you not to hear the alarm and result in your oversleeping and missing your morning meeting. It has happened to me on several occasions over the years. Second, as you know, with a wind-up clock, the alarm stays on for only a limited time and then sort of grinds to a stop when it has unwound itself. The result? If you are not completely awake by the time the alarm has finished, you miss another morning meeting. Third, I prefer to wake up slowly and do not like loud noises to wake me up. They give me a headache all morning. Because the clock is under the bed, when the alarm goes off, I am forced to jump out of bed quickly, get down on my hands and knees, search for the clock, and shut the alarm off. This is not the way I prefer to wake up. Besides, on a cold winter morning it forces me to jump right back into the warm bed. Finally, if I want to give myself 10 extra minutes of sleep, I have to find my glasses in order to be able to turn the little white hand all the way around and then try to guess how long 10 minutes would be in order to reset the alarm. By the time I do all of these things, I no longer feel like an additional snooze.

One night a few years ago I was on the road with my friend Marty. We were having a cocktail in the hotel bar late one evening, and I happened to mention to him the situation with my alarm clock.

He told me that my troubles were over and pulled from his attache case a digital alarm clock. He illustrated a few of the tricks of this technological marvel and convinced me to go to the nearest store and ask for a digital travel alarm clock when I returned home. I was sold.

Within a few days I had purchased my first (and as it turned out, my only) digital travel alarm clock. I remember it resembled a woman's cigarette case, very slim and attractive.

The young woman at the store was very helpful. She was even nice enough to set the clock at the correct time. She explained that I was purchasing the "best" travel alarm clock available. In hindsight, the word *best* should have been a warning to me. I should have inquired how something that only wakes me up in the morning can be the best at doing that. How could it be more dependable, better, more accurate, and so on, than what I already had? Except for a loud tick, nothing could be better than what I already had.

I took it home and put it in my shaving kit. I was looking forward to using it on my next trip, which was only a few days away. Coincidentally, I would be working with Marty again.

It was almost 11:00 P.M. in the hotel bar when I told Marty that I was tired and was going to retire to my room, set my new travel alarm clock for 6:15, and wake up refreshed and ready to go for our meeting in the morning.

After a shower I sat on the edge of my bed and took my new alarm clock out of its box. All I needed to do was to set the alarm for 6:15 A.M. I remember pressing a button and the clock flashed 4:30 P.M. I thought to myself, "I wonder what this is?" Upon closer inspection, I found out it was "Time in Another Time Zone." I can remember saying out loud, "This is supposed to be a travel alarm clock. Who cares what time it is in another time zone."

As best I could, I pressed some other buttons and thought I had set the alarm for 6:15 A.M. It was now about 11:30 P.M. Being tired, I went right to sleep.

When I heard the "beep-beep, beep-beep," I sat up in bed. I shut the alarm off and looked at the time. The clock was flashing 12:00 P.M. I had been asleep for half an hour.

Obviously I had done something wrong. I pressed that other button again and it flashed 5:00 P.M. I said to myself, "Maybe it's 6:15 A.M. wherever it is 5:00 P.M. now, in Taiwan or Korea or wherever the clock was manufactured. But here in Pennsylvania it's midnight. I know what I'll do. I'll neuter the other time zone." I pressed the buttons until the "Time in Another Time Zone" was 0:00. Now as far as my clock was concerned, there was only one place in the entire universe—Pennsylvania. I reset the alarm for 6:15 A.M. and went back to sleep.

When I heard "beep-beep, beep-beep" again, I sat up in bed. I shut the alarm off and looked at the time. The clock was flashing 1:00 A.M.

At this point I was getting upset. I took the page of directions out of the box and sat in the middle of the bed with my legs folded. I read every direction, reneutered the "Time in Another Time Zone," reset the alarm, and went back to sleep.

When the alarm went off at 2:00 A.M., I slammed the clock shut and threw it into my suitcase. I wanted to call Marty down the hall and tell him to come get the clock. Instead I called the front desk for a 6:15 wake-up call. I had a headache the entire morning.

Upon returning home, I took the clock back to the nice young woman that sold it to me.

"Didn't you tell me that this was a travel alarm clock?" I inquired. "Yes," she replied. "Then I was wondering why this button is here," I said. "Oh, that lets you know what time it is in some other time zone," she said.

"That's the point," I said. "If I'm sleeping, what do I care what time it is in some other time zone? All I need this clock to do is to wake me up in the morning, which is what I thought a travel alarm clock is supposed to do.

Why is this feature in the clock? It's not necessary and only confuses me.''

Her response told me much about what I had purchased. She said, ''I guess they could design it into the clock, so they figured why not design it into the clock.'' I didn't know how to respond, but I also knew that what she had said was important.

''Well,'' I said, ''that really isn't my problem. I am not the greatest when it comes to high-tech gadgets, and I can't figure out how to operate the alarm. I set it for 6:15 A.M., but it goes off every hour.''

Never tell a customer your product is ''the best''
until you know what they plan to use it for.

''Oh, that's another feature of this clock,'' she replied with great enthusiasm. ''Oh my God,'' I thought.

''Haven't you ever sat next to someone at a meeting or in the movies who has a digital watch that automatically beeps every hour to let them know that an hour has passed?'' she asked. I told her I had and that I never thought very much of the idea. ''Well, your clock has the same feature,'' she said.

''That's it!'' I said, ''I want my money back. Who needs a travel alarm clock that gives me time in another time zone and goes off every hour?''

I tried to explain to her that the clock had a serious problem as far as I was concerned; it did everything I didn't need it to do and didn't do what I needed it to do.

After refunding my money and apologizing, she said, ''I don't understand sir. This is *the best* travel alarm clock that we carry.''

The customer was wrong again. I guess I should have asked for their worst travel alarm clock. All it probably would have done is wake me up in the morning.

Now when I wind up my old travel clock, I gently caress it.

Lesson #8

Customers Do Not Buy Your Products or Services—They Buy Solutions to Their Problems.

Nine

There Is a Point of No Return

"Do not kick down the ladder by which you climbed."

C. H. Spungeon

There was once a woman I knew who enjoyed cooking chili for large numbers of people. They would all flock to her house especially during the Christmas season for some of her delicious chili. For several years I was one of those people.

One year I decided that to show my gratitude for such delicious chili and to ensure that the ritual would continue I would buy her the largest copper chili pot I could find as a gift. Since I know nothing about cooking and even less about cookware, I decided to wait until a local store had a cookware sale. In fact, I wasn't even sure you could cook chili in a copper pot.

Several months later I noticed an advertisement for a cookware sale at a local store. That evening I went to the store. There were copper pots of every shape, size, and variety in a huge display. I found the largest pot I could find but knew that before I bought it I needed to find out whether it was an appropriate pot for cooking chili since I had never cooked chili in my life. I went looking for a salesperson.

When I located a salesperson, she was talking on the telephone. It became obvious that she was talking to a customer so I didn't mind waiting. I think the entire conversation took 10 minutes. When she hung up, she came toward me but didn't say, "May I help you?" or "Sorry to keep you waiting."

I was about to ask my question when she said, "You wouldn't believe the stupid questions customers ask." I was stunned for a moment and didn't say anything. I sure as hell wasn't going to ask one of those stupid questions that customers ask. So I told her I didn't need any help, thanked her, and left the store.

Walking to my car, I thought about how many times a day something like this happens across the country, employees unknowingly committing murder on the customers. Management knew nothing of what happened although the store had just lost a sale. The employee still has her job today, probably with a merit increase.

While I had no particular desire to return to the store, about six months later I had no choice—a friend was getting married, and the bride was registered at the store. As I headed for the bridal department, I purposely went through the housewares department. As I expected, the same employee was behind the counter, probably still unknowingly killing the business.

After talking with someone called a bridal consultant, I identified the pattern of crystal the bride was collecting. Because they were such good friends of mine, I wanted to buy them a complete set of one particular glass. The consultant told me that no one had yet purchased iced tea glasses. I didn't know they made special glasses for iced tea, but I said I'll take 12 of them. She pointed to the area of the store where they would be located.

After searching for a few minutes, I located what appeared to be the pattern I was looking for. Since all the patterns looked alike to me and I could only find eight glasses in the pattern I thought I wanted, I thought it best to look

---

It's what employees do when their manager is not around that ultimately determines how effective the manager will be.

---

for a salesperson. I gingerly picked up the eight glasses and carried them with their stems between my fingers until I saw a cash register. I gently laid the eight crystal glasses on the counter. The woman behind the counter was (yes) talking on the telephone.

But unlike my friend in the housewares department who was talking with a customer, it became obvious after a while that this woman was talking to a friend, unless a customer had called to inquire about the recipe for twice-baked potatoes.

For 10 minutes I learned how to make twice-baked potatoes—how to scoop out the potato, how much sour cream and chives to use, and how to rebake them. I was hoping it was only going to be a one-course dinner.

I recalled my chili-pot experience in this same store and began to boil a little. I thought, "Here I am with eight crystal glasses at $40 a pop, looking for four more, and the salesperson has not acknowledged I am even at the counter."

When she moved into the complexities of a three-bean salad, I knew it was time for me to go. Besides, she was making me hungry. I turned and began to walk away. The only thing this salesperson ever said to me was when I walked away. With her hand over the telephone receiver, she said, "Sir, you're not going to leave those crystal glasses on the counter, are you?" I did not acknowledge what she said and continued to walk out of the store.

I did not stop at the manager's office. I did not make a scene. But I did solemnly promise myself that under no conditions would I ever return to that store. I have also told every friend I have about my experiences with this store. But note that management knows nothing of what happened. If they are judging their effectiveness as managers on how many customer complaints they get, they are living in a dream world. Most customers are nice customers. They never complain no matter what kind of service they get. They never kick, nag, or criticize in a public place like some people do.

But let me tell you what they will do. They will tell between 10 to 20 people of their experience, and management will never suspect a thing. And most important, they will exercise their right to vote; they will never go back. That is why we must never forget that, *when you lose a customer because of poor service chances are you will never know it.*

Lesson #9

A Great Many Customers Will Not Return Bad Service With Bad Behavior. They Are Always Polite and Never Get Loud, Cause a Scene, or Scream for the Manager. They Just Never Come Back.

Ten

To Have the Winning Hand in a Losing Game

"Take care of the ends and the means will take care of themselves."

Gandhi

This essay concludes with a lesson that we can think of as the lesson we must learn from the previous nine lessons—a kind of "megalesson" on customer satisfaction.

The essay also differs somewhat from the previous essays in that it does not tell a story. Instead, it presents a way of looking at customer satisfaction that enables us to identify the specific factors that satisfy and dissatisfy our customers. It is also implementable because it allows us to decide which components of the relationship must be improved before any improvements in customer satisfaction can be attained.

It will take the position that, from the customer's point of view, the major priority of most service organizations should be to make the customer's experience with them a neutral one—a wash; to create the least amount of customer dissatisfaction among all of their competitors.

Anyone interested in the subject of quality customer service is undoubtedly familiar with many of the definitions that are around: "Quality service is whatever the customer says it is," or "Quality service is meeting or exceeding customer expectations." In addition to being difficult to operationalize, these definitions assume that there is a continuum of customer satisfaction:

Figure 1   Traditional View of Customer Satisfaction

Worst Condition		Best Condition
• ◄───────────────────────────► •		
Dissatisfaction		Satisfaction

The continuum ranges from dissatisfaction to satisfaction, and, at some point after the customer's expectations have been met, they became satisfied customers. Before reaching that point, they experience varying degrees of dissatisfaction.

But customers know that it is not this simple—it is possible for them to not be satisfied but also to not be dissatisfied. In other words, customers know that the opposite of dissatisfaction is not satisfaction but simply the absence of dissatisfaction. And the opposite of satisfaction is not dissatisfaction but simply the lack of satisfaction.

As we shall see, understanding and implementing this important distinction is critical to achieving customer satisfaction. Otherwise we could easily be investing resources to improve the wrong components of customer satisfaction.

BACKGROUND

Over 30 years ago psychologist Frederick Herzberg developed an approach to employee satisfaction and motivation that differed somewhat from the then-accepted view.[1] At the time, employee satisfaction was also viewed as a

---

A good place to start for many businesses should be to seek to upset less customers than the competition.

---

single continuum ranging from dissatisfaction to satisfaction. The assumption was that, as management increased salaries, fringe benefits, job security, and so on, workers would become more satisfied and motivated.

Herzberg disagreed. He said that there were actually two separate continuums or two separate groups of factors that influenced employee satisfaction and motivation. One group, which has become known as *dissatisfiers,* causes much dissat-

---

[1] F. Herzberg, B. Mausner, and B. Snyderman, *The Motivation to Work* (New York: John Wiley & Sons, 1959). B. Gelb, "How Marketers of Intangibles Can Raise the Odds for Consumer Marketing," *Journal of Services Marketing,* Summer 1987, pp. 11–17, suggests the usefulness of Herzberg's work to the marketing of services but in a somewhat different manner from the one presented here.

isfaction among employees when they are not present but provides little or no satisfaction if they are present, (e.g., good salary, good working conditions, job security, good relationships with supervisors and peers, etc.). The factors in the second group, which has become known as *satisfiers*, lead to high levels of satisfaction and motivation when they are present but result in little or no dissatisfaction when they are not present (e.g., recognition, achievement, opportunities for personal growth, etc.).

A DIFFERENT LOOK AT CUSTOMER SATISFACTION WITH SERVICE

Can this 30-something-year-old explanation of employee satisfaction help those of us interested in customer satisfaction with our service? Consider the following three service encounters:

1. Your family is flying home from a two-week vacation. You rush but make your connecting flight in Chicago and land in your hometown close to on-time. Your luggage arrives on the same plane as you do. You pick up your luggage in the baggage claim area, leave the airport, and take a taxi home.

What would your reaction be to this experience? Most likely, there would be no reaction. There would be no letter of praise to the airline. The next day at work you would talk about your vacation. The flight experience would be a nonevent.

2. In addition to what happened in the encounter above, the following also occurred. The pilot came off the flight deck and invited your children in for a visit. A flight attendant gave them their own set of wings,

plus a puzzle book for children. When the flight arrived late in Chicago, an airline agent volunteered to call ahead to your departure gate to tell them you were on your way and asked for your baggage claim checks so he could inform the baggage handlers to ensure that your luggage would also make the connecting flight.

What would your reaction be to this experience? Most likely it would be extremely positive, maybe mixed with some surprise. There might be a letter of praise to the airline, perhaps mentioning some employees by name. The next day at work, you might talk as much about the flight experience as about your vacation.

3. Your flight arrives late into Chicago and you sprint a half mile to your connecting flight on the same airline only to see the plane pulling away from the gate as you nearly collapse at the counter. You can't help but recall that whenever you are a passenger on this airline they always make you sit and wait for "a few connecting passengers." But they always leave on time when you are the connectee. You wonder if there is a conspiracy.

You wait in Chicago for the next flight and arrive in your hometown five hours later. After viewing the luggage parade for 20 minutes, you find that your bags did not arrive. You wait in another line, only to be told your luggage will arrive on the first flight the following morning.

What would your reaction be to this experience? Most likely you would be extremely dissatisfied, possibly even outraged. There might be an irate letter to airline management, a solemn promise to yourself never to fly the airline again if you have a choice, and an increase in your diastolic blood pressure of 25 points. The next day at work the flight experience is the only thing that you talk about.

Based on the above three scenarios, the following seems evident:

1. There are some conditions in every service encounter that operate primarily to dissatisfy customers when they are present. However, the absence of these conditions does not create or build strong customer satisfaction. Like Herzberg, let's call these *dissatisfiers*. In the past many of these were thought of by service managers as factors that satisfy customers when in reality they are much more potent as dissatisfiers. That is, when they are not present, the best you can do is achieve no dissatisfaction among customers. The continuum for this group of factors is shown in Figure 2.

Figure 2   Customer Dissatisfiers

Worst Condition		Best Condition
• ◄─────────────────────────────────► •		
Dissatisfaction		No Dissatisfaction

In our airline example, passengers might identify the following as potential dissatisfiers: late flights, insufficient time to make connecting flights in hub airports, and luggage mishaps. When these factors are present, as in our third scenario, the airline has produced much dissatisfaction. However, when they are not present, as in our first scenario, the airline has produced no dissatisfaction.

2.   There are some conditions in every service encounter that, when present, can build high levels of customer satisfaction. However, if these conditions are not present, they do not prove highly dissatisfying to the customer. Let's call these *satisfiers* because they are capable of building high levels of customer satisfaction and, if they are not present, the worst you can do is to achieve no satisfaction. The continuum for this group of factors is shown in Figure 3.

Figure 3   Customer Satisfiers

Worst Condition		**Best Condition**
• No Satisfaction	←——————————→	• Satisfaction

In our airline example we might include the following satisfiers: flight-deck tours and puzzle books for the kids, help in making close flight connections, and executing swift luggage transfers. When these occur, as in our second scenario, the result is an extremely satisfied and happy passenger. However, when they do not occur, as in our first scenario, the worst that the airline can achieve is no satisfaction.

In summary, the critical point for managers to understand is that service is a *means* to achieving the *end* of customer satisfaction. Thus, it is important to focus on the *end* and not the *means*; that is, to determine the specific components of customer satisfaction and dissatisfaction. Otherwise, as we mentioned previously, we could be investing to improve the wrong things.

IDENTIFYING THE FACTORS

Obviously, for this approach to work, the dissatisfiers and satisfiers in the service encounter must be identified. You should be able to obtain this information with relative ease. And it should be obtained from customers as well as those employees who deal with customers on a daily basis.

Dissatisfiers

To identify the factors that are potential dissatisfiers, determine the following:

> What are the specific factors in the service encounter that operate primarily to upset customers when they are present, but the absence of which only results in customers not being upset?

For example, some of my personal dissatisfiers are: lost luggage, late shipments, long lines in hotels, having to repeat a request or problem to several employees, mistakes in my accounts (at a store, bank, etc.), and no cash in the automatic teller.

You might want to think of the dissatisfiers as "losers" because they are the causes of losing customers. They are the "must dos and don'ts" of the service encounter.

Satisfiers

To identify the factors that are potential satisfiers, determine the following:

> What are the specific factors in the service encounter
> that please and delight the customer when they are
> present, but the absence of which only results in cus-
> tomers not being pleased and delighted?

For example, some of my personal satisfiers are: help in fa-
cilitating a change of planes after a late arrival at a hub airport, an employee personally assuring me that my order
will be shipped on time and giving me their name, and a full
ice bucket when I enter my hotel room.

You may want to think of the satisfiers as "keepers" because, when customers are highly satisfied, motivated, and
loyal, there is a high tolerance for problems arising from the
dissatisfiers. They can cause customers to stay even when
bad things happen. However, customers are more likely to
leave when bad things happen in the absence of satisfiers.

IMPLEMENTATION

Viewing customer satisfaction in the way suggested provides some important and specific strategic and tactical advantages:

> 1. Concentrate first on identifying and then eliminat-
> ing the causes of dissatisfaction because, as we men-
> tioned, these are what cause customers to leave. And
> remember, preventing customer dissatisfaction is a
> prerequisite to achieving satisfaction. That is why
> your first quality-improvement goal should be to cre-
> ate the least amount of customer dissatisfaction
> among all of your competitors. Thus, satisfying cus-
> tomers truly involves gaining the winning hand in a
> losing game. You want to continually lose less cus-
> tomers than the competition.

2. Because dissatisfiers and satisfiers are two distinct groups of factors, you will not create satisfied customers by spending more money to reduce dissatisfaction. This is a critical point. It tells us that, if the dissatisfiers are improved beyond a certain point, no concurrent increase in customer satisfaction will occur. For example, spending money on a new phone system to cut waiting time from four rings to two rings, or to significantly improve airline snacks may have no impact on customer satisfaction.

3. Ask yourself the following question: Is this service capable of providing a great amount of customer satisfaction? Can physical and dental examinations, retail banking transactions, bus trips, and automatic teller transactions provide lots of satisfaction? Or is the best you can do causing no dissatisfaction? You may be forced to admit that satisfaction is not likely and that your goal should be to make the service experience a neutral one for the customer—a wash.

4. Having eliminated opportunities for dissatisfaction, you can devote resources to satisfying and delighting your customers after you have determined that such opportunities exist and what they are.

Lesson #10

Customers Cannot Be Satisfied Until after They Are Not Dissatisfied. Your First Service Priority Should Be to Eliminate All the Opportunities for Dissatisfying Customers, because They Are What Cause Customers to Leave. Then You Can Invest in Satisfying and Delighting Them.

CHECKLIST FOR PART I
Lessons from Customers
about Satisfying Customers

▼

✔ There are only two conditions under which customers will change their behavior: (1) when it's a matter of life and death (and even then not in every case), and (2) if they want to—if they are given a reason to change.

✔ Our needs usually come in clusters, not in bits and pieces. The best organizations organize themselves to satisfy clusters of customer needs.

✔ Customers should never be inconvenienced because of company policies that are known only to employees—and do not become known to customers until they are used against them.

✔ Customers should never be required to restate their request or complaint to several employees before having it resolved.

✔ If you establish negative expectations for your customers, you will always meet them.

✔ Quality service means never having to say, "That's not my job."

✔ The delivery of quality service is never the customer's job.

✔ Customers do not buy your products or services—they buy solutions to their problems.

✔ A great many customers will not return bad service with bad behavior. They are always polite and never get loud, cause a scene, or scream for the manager. They just never come back.

✔ Customers cannot be satisfied until after they are not dissatisfied. Your first service priority should be to eliminate all the opportunities for dissatisfying customers, because they are what cause customers to leave. Then you can invest in satisfying and delighting them.

PART
II

What Customers Know about Managing People

Eleven

Beware of Employees Doing Their Work

"Never give an order that can't be obeyed."

General Douglas MacArthur

Whenever I visit a strange city, I usually try to arrive sometime during the afternoon of the day before I am expected to be there so as not to be rushed. I often go to a local mall to visit the bookstores and music stores where I usually purchase a book or tape to bring back to my hotel room.

On one particular visit it was only a $2.90 cab ride from my hotel to the mall. I browsed for about an hour and was ready to return to the hotel. I noticed that I only had a $50 bill and realized that I had better get it changed because a cab driver would not likely be able to change it. And if he were, he probably wouldn't be too happy about it for a $2.90 fare.

I recall it was 4:50 P.M. as I approached the mall exit and noticed a branch bank just to the left of the door. "How fortunate," I thought to myself, "I still have 10 minutes." I noticed that there were two tellers working, one had four people in her line, the other one had none. "Boy, what luck," I thought as I walked up to the teller with no line.

I pushed my $50 across her counter and said, "Could I please have change for this $50 bill?" "I'm sorry" she responded, "but you will have to go to the next window." I looked at my watch and replied, "But the branch is still open for another 10 minutes, isn't it?"

With that she lowered her head and leaned across the counter in order to get very close to me. "I'm counting down," she whispered to me. I had never heard that expression so I whispered back, "To what? If this mall is going to blow up or something, I want to get out of here."

What she said to me next was a surprise to say the least. She said, "I'm fairly new, and our branch manager doesn't like to stay much past 5 o'clock. So he has instructed me to start balancing my drawer at 4:45 and to send all the customers to the next window where the teller is much more experienced than I am. She only takes a few minutes to balance her drawer and we're outta here by 5:10 at the latest."

I couldn't believe a manager would say such a thing to an employee, and then she compounds the crime by telling it to a customer. As I was waiting in the line at the next window, I thought that in my case such antics really didn't matter because I was not a customer of the bank. Since I was a transient, who cares what I think of this organization? But, you see, *the employee did not know this.* For all she knew, I could have had $150,000 on deposit and numerous other relationships with the bank.

I did not realize what a profound lesson in management I had just learned at this branch bank until a few weeks later when I arrived at a big-city airport to catch a 7 A.M. flight back home.

The ropes were up at the airline ticket counter to guide the passengers through a maze to the next available agent. Fortunately for me there was no one in line. So I bypassed the maze and went directly up to the ticket counter.

As I handed the agent my ticket, she said, "Sir, you will have to go through the line." I thought she was joking, but

---

No one likes to fail, and unfortunately managers often unwittingly set up employees to fail in the eyes of the customer.

I looked back to my left and right and said, "There isn't any line." With that she became a little firmer and said, "Please sir, I have been instructed that I cannot wait on you unless you come through the line."

Keeping calm, I thought to myself, "Maybe we are on 'Candid Camera.'" So I retraced my steps back through the maze, making a couple of left turns and right turns and came to a stop by the sign that read "Please Wait for the Next Available Agent." Sure enough, she looked up at me and said, "Next!"

Sitting on the plane, I recalled what had happened to me at the bank. Both incidents have some important similarities.

First, the employee was not at fault in either one. While it is easy to blame the employee when such incredible things happen, it is management who has set the employee up to fail. And no one likes to fail. Second, these things happen because management is confusing the "work" of the unit and the employees with the "job" of the unit and the employees. And they are communicating either implicitly or explicitly that the work is more important than the job. Finally, both incidents illustrate clearly that, when an employee is forced to choose between the two, they will choose the one which they believe management values most.

From time to time we all need to be reminded to separate our *job* from the *work* that we do and to never forget which one is more important.

Lesson #11

*Never Allow an Employee's Work
to Interfere with His Job.*

Twelve

Care for More than Your Customers

"Fail to honor people, they fail to honor you."

Lao Tzu

A few years ago an elderly relative suffered a severe stroke. She was rushed to the hospital where her life was in danger for several days. After about five days she began to make miraculous improvements, and the doctors were encouraged.

After another five days of continued improvement relatives were advised that little more could be done for her at the hospital. They were advised to either place her in a nursing home or, on the slight chance that she could improve further, consider the possibility of placing her in a physical therapy facility for a period of intensive treatment.

At that time a decision could be made as to whether to place her in a nursing home or to allow her to return home.

The family discussed the alternatives and decided that, before a decision was made, she should be examined by a specialist in physical therapy. A specialist was retained whose opinion was that she could benefit from a two-week intensive physical therapy program. A physical therapy facility that was located approximately 70 miles from the hospital was selected. The patient, in her mid-70s and only 10 days after suffering a major stroke, was placed in an ambulance and shipped to the facility.

Upon arrival she was placed in a wheelchair and wheeled to the receiving area. After sitting in the receiving area for two and a half hours, she was told that she could not be admitted because some of her paperwork had not been completed by the staff at the hospital. She was placed back in the ambulance and driven another 70 miles back to the hospital. Fortunately a room was available and she was put back in bed. The only thing this elderly stroke victim had accomplished for the day was a 140-mile ambulance ride and a two-and-a-half-hour wait in a wheelchair.

For better or for worse I had decided to visit her that evening. I live 1,000 miles away, and after two plane rides I arrived fully expecting to rent a car at the airport and drive to the physical therapy facility. Fortunately I called family members from the airport and was told she was back at the hospital. They also related the above details of her day in the health-care industry. I was livid as I drove from the airport to the hospital.

When I arrived at the hospital, I demanded to speak with everyone who had anything to do with what happened: physicians, administrators, floor nurses, social workers, and physical therapists. I had only two questions: What happened? and Who was responsible?

Needless to say, I did not receive any definitive answers to either question. However, I did find out a great deal of other information. For example, one staff member told me that foreign doctors are always bad when it comes to paperwork, and that it was unfortunate that the hospital has so many foreign doctors. The medical staff blamed the administrative staff. Two nurses told me I should write an article on how overworked and underpaid they were. One nurse pointed the finger at a social worker. The social worker spent most of her time using the latest psychological techniques to get me to calm down. She also told me

---

Customers sense very quickly when employees really do not want to be a part of the organization.

---

something I already knew—because of what happened, I had a great deal of frustration and anger in me that I should release. So I did. I was expecting her to recommend that I read *How to Be Your Own Best Friend*. Finally someone even mentioned the driver of the ambulance as the guilty party.

After more than two hours of frustration and often-heated conversations, the best they could come up with was that no one knew for sure what had happened and no one was responsible. It was just ''one of those things,'' and several people seemed to hint that something was wrong with me because I was so upset about an elderly woman with a stroke having to ride 140 miles and sit two and a half hours in a wheelchair for nothing.

I headed for the parking lot in need of some therapy myself. In fact, the social worker seemed to hint strongly that such was the case. I wish she had been as concerned about my relative's physical health as she pretended to be about my mental health.

As I drove to my motel, I recounted the appalling events of the day. Obviously I was upset about the care my relative was receiving. But beyond that I was overwhelmed by what I had just gone through with the staff of the hospital. During the entire time I spent with the employees of the hospital, two things became apparent: First, not once did anyone ever say a supportive thing about another employee or unit of the hospital. It was clear that the medical staff thought very little of the administrative staff and vice versa. Both the medical staff and the administrative staff seemed to have little regard for the social workers. Second, not once did anyone ever say a positive thing about the hospital itself. I sensed that no one I had met was glad they worked there.

Sitting in my motel room, I thought to myself, ''With what you have just witnessed, why should you be surprised at what happened today? Under these conditions, what other level of care could you expect?''

I began to hope that similar conditions did not exist at the motel I was staying in. If the front desk, housekeeping, and food service departments in the motel got along like those at the hospital, I would probably be safer sleeping in the car.

Lesson #12

*You Will Never Treat Your
Customers Any Better than You
Treat Each Other.*

Thirteen

The Medicine Man Is a Manager

"Don't equate activity with efficiency."

Harvey Mackey

Professionals other than managers must also face customers daily. For example, physicians deal with their customers (patients) everyday. Before too long patients come to realize that physicians have a management skill that many managers need to develop.

During the course of their medical school training they apparently are taught to classify the situations they face in their everyday work environment into one of two categories: (1) those that they will be able to cure or fix, and (2) those that they will be unable to cure or fix. Why is this distinction so important? Because it enables them to bring the appropriate expertise to bear on each category, thereby maximizing their contribution to the patient's well-being. There is an important analogy here for managers and their customers.

For example, a physician determines very quickly whether a patient has a medical problem or a medical condition. A problem could be a broken bone, appendicitis, or tonsillitis. A condition could be an allergy, chronic sinusitis, or a certain skin disorder.

The distinction between a problem and a condition is an important one to a physician. Medical problems can be "cured or fixed." The physician may have to review

---

While most managers are trained as problem solvers, the majority of situations they now face resemble more what a physician would describe as a "condition."

---

several possible complex solutions with long and involved recuperation times, but once a cure is selected the physician knows with a high degree of certainty what the outcome will be. After the necessary recuperation time everything will be basically the same as it was before the problem occurred.

However, for a medical condition the physician knows that it cannot be cured or fixed. And both the physician and the patient know that everything will never be as it was before the condition arose. The physician does not try to cure or fix a medical condition. Instead he or she "treats" the condition, often with the help of the patient. Together they try to constantly fine-tune and maintain a delicate balance so the patient can function normally.

For our purposes it is important to note that a physician will *never* try to cure a medical condition because he or she knows that conditions cannot be cured and that trying to do so is a waste of both time and money.

A MANAGER'S PROBLEMS AND CONDITIONS

Can the idea of problems and conditions be useful to managers? The answer is *yes*. It seems that the majority of managers have been educated and trained to perceive themselves as problem solvers. They are there to solve the problems of the business.

Examples include replacing a department manager that just resigned, locating a new sales office, investing in new plant and equipment, and deciding whether to add a new wing to the school. Like solving medical problems, solving management problems might take time, require a great deal of analysis, and be very complex. But once the solution has been decided upon, the decision made, the new manager hired, the sales office located, and the piece of equipment selected, the problem is solved. Like medical problems, management problems have solutions *or at least* specific end points where decisions must be made.

But when managing people, managers face another set of circumstances that are really not problems. They have no solutions or specific end points where decisions must be made.

Examples include encouraging peak performance from all employees, changing an organization's culture, improving product or service quality, improving productivity, or designing a flatter, leaner, and more flexible organization structure. These and similar situations are not problems in the medical sense, they are conditions. They are a lot like allergies and psoriasis—they never go away. A manager cannot cure or fix them, and it is here that managers can learn something from their physicians.

The lesson is this: Physicians cure medical problems and treat medical conditions. *Cure* is another word for *solve,* and *treat* is another word for *manage.* Therefore, *managers must solve the problems of their job and manage the conditions of their job.*

The key, of course, is to know the difference. It's clear that physicians do, but not clear that many managers do, especially since most managers have been trained to be decision makers—to gather whatever information is available or necessary, develop alternatives, select an alternative, make a decision, and seek closure. As a result, we see many managers doing something their doctor would never do: They try to cure conditions. For example, I know:

- A corporate planning officer who tried to "cure" the condition of strategic planning by purchasing a copy of a particular business best-seller for all corporate officers.

- A retail banker who tried to "cure" the condition of implementing a relationship marketing philosophy in the bank by simply changing the title of the installment lending officers to personal bankers.

- A college administrator who tried to "cure" the condition of recruiting and maintaining a quality liberal arts faculty by reorganizing the college.

- A marketing director of a credit union who tried to "cure" the condition of developing and nurturing a selling philosophy throughout the organization by issuing specific sales goals to customer contact personnel without a moment's training in selling techniques.

- A human resource director who tried to "cure" the condition of motivating peak performance by purchasing a copy of a business best-seller with a 60-second solution for all sales office managers.

SEPARATE YOUR PROBLEMS FROM YOUR CONDITIONS

Doing what the managers in the preceding scenarios did and nothing more is a waste of time and money. Like good physicians, good managers must separate the problems of their job from the conditions of their job.

It is a critical skill because:

1. The newest and most frustrating parts of the 1990s' manager's job are the conditions they must now manage. Also when the manager is under pressure, it is often very tempting to try to apply a cure, a solution, and often a quick fix. However, product and service quality, strategic planning, peak employee performance, changing the organization's culture, and similar conditions cannot be cured or solved. They do not go away.

2. Treating conditions will not require problem-solving methods such as statistical decision-making techniques, computer decision models, or financial control methods. No, treating conditions will require

management and leadership in the truest sense. Like medical conditions, the conditions we now face require constant attention, fine-tuning and maintaining a delicate balance, as well as the realization that everything will never be as it was before the condition arose.

Lesson #13

Do What Any Good Physician Does: Separate the Problems of Your Job from the Conditions of Your Job, and Never Try to Cure a Condition.

Fourteen

We Don't Know What It Is, but We Love It When We Get It

"You just set the work before the men and have them do it."

Henry Ford

Very early one morning a few years ago I boarded the first of four flights in Seattle. I was bound for Lexington, Kentucky, by way of Salt Lake City, Dallas, and Atlanta. I was hungry and was hoping for some breakfast. I asked a flight attendant if breakfast was being served, and she said only orange juice, coffee, and peanuts were available. Since I ordinarily don't eat peanuts for breakfast, I declined.

I boarded the next flight in Salt Lake City, which would take me to Dallas. By now I was very hungry. Unfortunately, the only food served on the flight was peanuts.

As the time zones changed, my desire for more substantial food increased. I was sure that the change of planes in Dallas for my flight to Atlanta would bring with it a meal. Unfortunately, because of another time zone change, I had missed another mealtime for airlines. But my stomach did not know it was changing time zones.

Trying to keep myself together, I decided to practice visualization. I concentrated on the popcorn I would have when I reached Atlanta. My expectations were set—I would get popcorn in the Atlanta airport.

We arrived a little late in Atlanta, and I had to hustle to my next gate. When I got there, everyone had already boarded the flight to Lexington. As I was checking in, I turned toward the snack area only to find a sparkling clean, empty, popcorn machine. The ramp agent made the mistake of asking me how I was. So I told him. In fact, I probably overtold him. He told me that, unfortunately, only peanuts would be served on the flight.

Sitting in my seat, I resigned myself to the fact that I was going to starve to death. I forgave everyone who had ever done anything to me.

Just as the door was about to be closed, the ramp agent came on the plane carrying a freshly popped, piping hot bag of microwave popcorn. I'm sure the other passengers wondered, "Who is this guy?" when he brought it to my seat. He had rushed to the flight crew lounge, which was equipped with a microwave oven and popcorn for use by flight crews between flights, and prepared the snack just for me.

What a wonderful employee he is for the airline. I was so impressed that I wrote a letter to the airline and told them so.

How many times does the typical customer have a similar experience with an organization? One where they say, "I'm going to get that person's name and write a letter to the company telling them what a great employee they have.'' Not very many if they're like me. In fact, they can probably remember each one they've had in the last few years.

I think it's safe to call such incidents ''peak performances.'' But more importantly, what do these peak-performance experiences have in common? If quality of service is an important issue, and it appears to be, then this question is an important one. As far as most customers can tell, most service employees are operating on minimums. The ramp agent in Atlanta was operating on maximums.

WHAT IS A PEAK PERFORMANCE?

What do all peak performances seem to have in common? In all that I can remember (and I suspect in all that you can remember), the employees *chose to do* what they did; they did not *have to do* what they did. The ramp agent would still have his job today at the same level of salary if he had chosen *not* to do what he did. He chose at that moment to perform far beyond what was necessary. No one was supervising him, measuring him, or looking over his shoulder. But when the need arose, he voted for the customer and the airline, not for himself.

After similar experiences, many managers ask, ''Why can't I get the people in my department to do that?'' or ''Why can't we hire people that do this?'' However, when asked what ''that'' or ''this'' is, they usually say something like ''I don't know what it is, but I know it when I see it.''

The Components of a Peak Performance

What is ''it''? The foundation of all peak employee performances is *discretionary effort*, the difference between the maximum amount of care and effort a person can bring to their job and the minimum amount necessary to keep from being penalized or reprimanded.[1] Thus, the formula for a peak performance is:

The Peak Performance Formula

$$\text{Acceptable performance} + \text{Discretionary effort} = \text{Peak performance}$$

Think about it. What a customer gets from an employee in a peak service encounter requires discretionary effort:

- The "choose-to-do" part of the job, not just the "have-to-do" part of the job (acceptable performance).
- The difference between the maximum possible and the minimum acceptable.
- The difference between what we know we can be and what we are.

What Are We Selling?

The concept of discretionary effort is a critical one for managers in service industries. It is the common denominator of peak performance. We must never forget that service businesses do not produce—they perform. They do not sell "things"; they sell human performances. The majority of complaints that come into GM are not aimed at people—they are aimed at products. But the majority of complaints that come into an airline, educational institution, health-

---

[1]The concept of discretionary effort was first suggested by Daniel Yankelovich and John Immerwahr in their *Putting the Work Ethic to Work* (New York: Public Agenda Foundation, 1983), p. 1. Their concept has been the catalyst for my ideas on peak performance.

care organization, or financial institution are not aimed at products—they are aimed at people.

This is the key difference between a front-line job in an automobile plant and a front-line job in a service business. A manufacturing plant is dominated by low-discretion jobs. The employee on an assembly line has little control or discretion over how much or how little effort is devoted to work. That was the genius of the assembly line. It took all the need for commitment, motivation, and creativity out of the job. In a low-discretion job, it really doesn't matter if an employee is satisfied, committed, or motivated, as lo .g as they do their job. An uncommitted, dissatisfied person in a

---

For knowledge workers there is often a big difference between the "have-to-do" part of a job and the "choose-to-do" part of a job.

---

low-discretion job probably has little negative impact on the organization. Low-discretion jobholders can be supervised into being effective.

This is not the case in service organizations. Service organizations are dominated by high-discretion jobs. Jobholders have a great amount of discretion or control over how much or how little effort is devoted to work. They are part of the new "knowledge workers," and they cannot be supervised into being effective. An unmotivated, uncommitted, dissatisfied person in a high-discretion job is an unmotivated organization. In other words, a rude flight attendant on a given day is a rude airline. An unprepared,

incompetent college professor or bank loan officer is an unprepared, incompetent college or bank, respectively.

A Different Kind of Work Force

Today's manager faces a different kind of work force. As a
result we cannot apply rust-bucket industry concepts of
quality control to service industries. Yes, airlines can measure on-time landings and lost luggage mishaps. Other service industries can measure and control how many times a
phone rings before it is answered, whether customer-
contact employees smile, and other easily measured aspects of service delivery. Unfortunately this is only acceptable performance. Customers expect their flight to be on
time, their luggage to arrive when they do, their bank statement to be correct and on time, and money to be in the cash
machine. However, they don't expect airline employees to
make popcorn for them or to hang up their garment bag.
And as we have seen, it is these discretionary acts of employees that constitute a peak service experience and ultimately create loyal customers.

When your services are the same, you will beat or lose to
your competition on the performances of your people. If
this truth is understood and appreciated, another one log-
ically follows: Acceptable performance is no longer acceptable. The ticket into the game is acceptable performance. The winner's edge will go to those organizations
where peak performance is the only acceptable
performance.

The implications for managers in service organizations
should be clear. Management can always control the *acceptable
performance* part of the peak performance formula. In a low-
discretion job this is the largest contributor to peak

performance. (In fact, they might be the same.) However, for a high-discretion job, acceptable performance is a much smaller contributor. While management can *control* acceptable performance, it can only *influence* discretionary effort. It can enforce and police acceptable performance, but must exhibit leadership to unleash the discretionary effort of high-discretion jobholders. We know that authority can produce acceptable performance, but only commitment produces discretionary effort.

When employees have to choose between the organization, the customer, and themselves, which one will prevail? The called-for action is not in their job description.

> *Most service businesses sell ''brown paper bags.''*
> *Thus, when your services are the same, you will*
> *win or lose on the performance of your people.*

They do not *have* to do it. If they *choose* to do it, if they vote for the organization or the customer, you have a performance culture, an organization where everyone does their best work.

ACHIEVING PEAK PERFORMANCE

Individual discretionary effort is a necessary condition for a performance culture. High-discretion employees doing their best work requires discretionary effort. Thus, managers in service organizations and service units desiring a performance culture must encourage peak performance and avoid doing things that discourage discretionary effort.

Encouraging Peak Performance

One way to think of the difference between the maximum possible and the minimum acceptable is as a commitment gap. Such a gap exists when employees operate at minimum levels because they do not have commitment to their job or to the organization.

What do knowledge workers want from their jobs? The Public Agenda Foundation found these top 10 qualities:[2]

(1) Working with people who treat me with respect.

(2) Interesting work.

(3) Recognition for good work.

(4) Chance to develop skills.

(5) Working with people who listen if you have ideas about how to do things better.

(6) A chance to think for myself rather than carry out instructions.

(7) Seeing the end results of my work.

(8) Working for efficient managers.

(9) A job that is not too easy.

(10) Feeling well informed about what is going on.

It is interesting to note that job security, benefits, and high pay did not make the top 10 (although they were in the top 15). Yet many middle managers who follow the low-discretion model still deal with employees as if security, benefits, and money are the only ways to encourage peak performance.

As was mentioned, a true performance culture is one in which everyone does their best work, and it is manage-

---

[2]Ibid., p. 23.

ment's responsibility to create the environment where everyone wants to and is able to do their best work. The following five actions will succeed in encouraging individual commitment and peak performance:

- Tie compensation directly to performance that enhances both the efficiency and effectiveness of the organization or unit.

- Give tangible and public recognition to people who perform beyond the acceptable level. (I was notified by the airline that the ramp agent's performance was recognized and rewarded.)

- Accept completely the idea that employees should share directly and significantly in overall productivity gains (however defined).

- Encourage joint participation (management and employees) in defining recognizable goals and standards against which individual performance can be judged.

- Provide special attention to as well as training to deal with the problems and difficulties that middle managers face in supporting and implementing programs of change in the organization.

Discouraging Peak Performance

Certain actions will discourage individual commitment:

- Allowing situations to develop where the interests of employees run counter to the well-being of the organization. For example, by introducing new technology in a way that threatens employees' job security or overtime; by introducing incentive pay systems that exclude groups whose efforts are needed to complete service delivery; or by pitting one group against another who are involved in serving the same customer group.

- Trying to increase productivity or improve service quality and not being prepared to accept the cost of doing it.

- Permitting a significant gap to develop between management rhetoric and the actual reward system. Nothing fuels employee cynicism more than management blindness about which employee behaviors are really important.

- Pretending or trying to mislead employees into believing that programs designed to increase productivity are actually intended to increase job satisfaction and employee morale; nothing breeds a greater mistrust of management.

- Providing perks, bonuses, or privileges for managers that widen the gap between them and those who do the work. Never provide management bonuses when some employees are being laid off.

In conclusion, it should be clear that the assembly-line, low-discretion management model is out of step with today's knowledge workers. These educated people want the satisfaction of knowing that their work is respected and was competently performed. Ultimately customers will know whether management is succeeding in producing commitment among high-discretion jobholders.

Lesson #14

The Most Important Parts of Employees' Contributions to the Goals of Your Organization Are Being Made at Their Discretion.

Fifteen

Everybody Wants to Be Somebody

"There are no bad regiments, only bad colonels."

Napoleon Bonaparte

Most businesses promote their products as if most customers are motivated by a drive toward their mental picture of themselves operating at their personal best (their "ideal self"). In other words, they assume that most customers really want to be all they can be. But how do most managers feel about their employees on this same issue? The answer to this question is an important one for a manager to ponder. It is important because the assumptions managers make about the people they manage will obviously influence the managerial approaches they use. This essay tells the story of three managers who believe that the people they manage really want to be the best they can be.

The first manager worked in the operations area of a brokerage firm. This is a "back-room" part of the business. No one in the department ever meets face-to-face with clients. Once I was visiting her at work and found a framed statement hanging on the wall behind her desk that read: "We deliver client-driven service that is unparalleled by any firm in any industry in the world."

Another time I was visiting a former student who had only recently been appointed the manager of the largest branch of her bank. She invited me into her office. After talking about old times she opened the middle drawer of her desk. Taped to the bottom of the drawer was the following: "The service we provide the customers of our branch will be demonstrably better than any branch of any bank in the city."

Finally, a few years ago I was conducting some group interviews for a research project I was working on. One particular group was made up entirely of bank CEOs, and the majority of our discussions had focused on the problems and difficulties of getting the best efforts of people. One CEO remained behind, however, to show me something he had in his wallet. It was a three-by-five folded index card on which he had typed: "We will become the best bank in the state for medium-size businesses by 1992."

Is there anything to be learned from what these managers are doing? Or are they just using a different or newer or softer kind of club with which to beat their employees?

We have known for many years that visualization is apparently a successful means of individual motivation. Psychologists and human-potential experts are pretty much convinced that people who set a goal and repeatedly visualize the accomplishment of it often achieve great things. They tell us envisioning our goals, writing them down, constantly referring to them throughout the day, and rehearsing our future is a self-development technique practiced by many achievement-oriented individuals as a method of self-motivation. In fact, there are many athletes, actors, actresses, and public speakers who have used these techniques successfully for years.

Is it possible that such techniques also may be applicable to groups? Apparently the above three managers believe they are. If such techniques are applicable to groups, they could be useful to managers who are faced with the task of getting better results from people—and fast.

Actually, we should not be surprised that effective managers have a vision, an image, of exactly what it is they want to do. In fact, there are those who agree that all the planning in the world is worthless unless there is first a vision of greatness.

Exactly what is a vision of greatness? It is at least two things:

- A clear image or picture of what you want your organization or part of the organization to be.

- A focus on what you want to achieve—not necessarily how it will be achieved.

This clear image of what you want is then used to organize and instruct every step toward its achievement. Note that the above three visions of greatness qualify on each dimension. They focus on what the business or unit of the business wants to be and provide very clear direction for managerial decision making.

Your organization or the part of the organization that you manage is headed somewhere. It almost certainly has momentum. If management does not consciously set the direction, then the direction or momentum must evolve out of everyday operating decisions. In fact, the direction will be nothing more than the sum total of your day-to-day operating decisions. So you have nothing to lose by developing your own "vision of greatness." That is, of course, if you believe that your people really want to be the best they can be.

A basic premise of the human-potential movement is that rehearsing our future or visualizing a desired goal can greatly improve individual performance. Some managers are successfully applying such techniques to groups.

Are there any guidelines for creating a vision of greatness? Among managers who believe that their people want to be the best they can be, three predictors of success appear repeatedly. The vision must be achievable and motivational and, most importantly, it must be a "crusade" for the customer.

1. *Make the vision achievable.* By acting on their view of what they believe is possible, and with a clear sense of purpose, the best managers seek to create a work environment in which: (a) other people can share management's commitment, (b) commitment is the norm, not the exception, and, as one manager told me, (c) "people want to do more than just show up for work."

But while the vision should "stretch" people toward greater performance, it must at the same time be realistic and achievable. In other words, it should open a vision of new opportunities of what could be, but it should not lead the organization or unit into ventures far beyond its capabilities.

2. *Make the vision motivational.* There seems to be unanimous belief in the motivational power of a vision of greatness. Apparently the image that such a vision creates inspires action and fuels motivation among other managers and employees.

It appears to provide a shared sense of purpose outside the day-to-day activities taking place within the organization or unit. Therefore, such end results as sales volume, return on investment, new accounts, market share, and expense reductions can be viewed as the result of the pursuit and achievement of a vision, and not the vision itself.

Otherwise, the numbers are the vision. When I asked the bank CEO what purpose his index card served, he replied, "It tells me and everyone else in the bank why we get up and come to work in the morning."

3. *Make the vision a crusade for customers.* Customers should be critical in focusing your vision. The best statements of vision do not mention end results such as profits, costs, sales volume, return on investment, market share, or the bottom line. As in the three visions cited earlier, many managers make them crusades for the customer, *a cause that is worth pursuing for its own sake.*

Commenting on her vision of service greatness, the bank branch manager told me, ''The only reward most employees usually get for all their efforts is that the bank makes more money. I believe people want to commit to something bigger, at least I do.''

There is no doubt that the efforts of employees are an important competitive weapon for any organization in today's environment. Having employees who are willing to go the extra mile for the organization or the customer when that extra mile is needed may make the difference.

So, if you believe that most people really want to be the best they can be, then it appears that what works to improve individual performance also may work to improve the performance of groups: a clear vision of what you want to become and constant reference to it.

When President John F. Kennedy declared: ''We will put a man on the moon before the end of the decade,'' all Americans clearly understood his picture of the future, and thousands of government employees couldn't wait to get up the next day to go help make it a reality.

Lesson #15

Most Employees Want to Commit to Something Bigger than the Numbers.

Sixteen

The People Who Write the Ads Don't Have to Meet the Customers

" 'Surprises' are a cardinal sin. See each business situation for what it is and not through one's emotional glasses of what one might like to see."

Reginald H. Jones

Recently, a friend of mine went into a bank to make a deposit and purchase some travelers checks. She was waiting in a line behind three or four other customers when another employee some distance away volunteered to wait on her. My friend was impressed and pleased by the employee's effort and was planning on thanking her before she left the bank.

After she had made her deposit, she mentioned that she wanted to buy some travelers checks. She could see a visible change come over the teller. My friend assumed that the teller was upset because she was about to inform her that

127

she would have to go and wait in another line for travelers checks.

Instead, the teller said, "That's just my luck. I volunteer to take somebody else's customer and they want travelers checks. I hate doing travelers checks!" Another customer had been murdered at the front line. When my friend related her experience to me, it reminded me of something a bank employee had told me a few years ago.

This bank employee also happens to be a friend of mine. He used to work in the branch office of a local bank. Although I do my banking business with a competitor, I occasionally stopped by to see him on my way home. I would drive up to the drive-in window, and say a few words, and drive on.

Like most banks, this one has over the years stressed in its advertising the high quality of service it provides to its customers. In addition, the friendliness and helpfulness of its customer-contact personnel are continually hammered into my head over the TV and radio as well as through the newspaper.

It was during one of these advertising campaigns that I decided to stop and see my friend. As I drove up to the window, I could see that he was not having a particularly good day. He was perspiring and had a frown on his face.

"Where are all the friendly, smiling, helpful people I just heard about on the radio?" I said smartly. "This certainly can't be the same bank that they were talking about. I'm obviously at the wrong bank. Excuse me!"

He knew that I was not serious. Nevertheless, what he said to me was very serious, and I have never forgotten it. He said, "I don't write the ads, and the people who do don't work out here!" What a statement on managing in a service business, on the realities of selling human performances, on the challenge of peak performance and discretionary effort, and on what this book is all about.

There are currently many executives in service industries who are pledging to their customers that quality is important. Unfortunately, in far too many cases, all that is involved for the executive is issuing directives and memos on the subject while expecting someone else to follow through. As my friend found out when she tried to purchase travelers checks, all of the advertising about quality service, friendly and helpful personnel, as well as all of the management memos, directives, and rhetoric, can be a waste of time, energy, and money if the front line doesn't believe it. We have seen this problem in several other places in this book. *The reality of what is delivered differs greatly from what management thinks reality is.*

Most managers know when change is necessary. In other words, they are skilled in identifying and diagnosing the need for change. However, while these skills are necessary they are not sufficient for effectively managing change in an organization.

Sooner or later, change must take place. That is, people somewhere in the organization (in a service organization it is usually those who deal with customers, clients, patients, or students) must change their behavior. They must either do something differently, or stop doing something and start doing something else. They must change their skills, attitudes, and behavior. And for this to happen, top managers must become directly involved in the change effort. They must actively and visibly support and defend the need for change or none will occur.

PREPARING TO IMPLEMENT CHANGE

Every organization is an ongoing entity with a history and a culture that favors the continuation of existing behavior and activities. Therefore, before trying to implement change in an organization, prepare yourself by: (1) assessing the climate for change, and (2) selecting a strategy for implementation. This preparatory work will reap high dividends later on.

Assessing the Climate for Change

There are three factors that will influence the outcome of any change effort in your organization, and they must be acknowledged prior to any attempt at change.

1. *The leadership climate in the organization.* Every organization has a work environment or climate that results from the leadership style and administrative practices of management. Any change, no matter the magnitude, that does not have the support and commitment of management has only a slim chance of success. Attempts at change fail many times when management assumes change is for everyone in the organization but them. Everything else in the process may be done correctly, but the critical ingredient is missing.

2. *The formal organization structure.* Any proposed change must be compatible with management philosophy, policies, systems of control, and the organization structure. Of course, some of these factors may be what management wants to change. The important point is that a change in one factor must be compatible with all the others. For example, trying to implement an innovative reward system in only one part of the organization will usually have effects outside that area and they will usually be negative ones.

3. *The organization culture.* Probably the best definition of the concept of organization culture that I have ever heard is, "It's the way we do things around here."

Culture is the web of values, shared beliefs, assumptions, and behaviors that employees of an organization acquire over time. In many ways it is similar to an individual's personality. It is the traditional way that people have always behaved at work. The title of this essay tells us clearly that any attempt at change that runs counter to the expectations and attitudes of employees is likely to be resisted. When there is a large discrepancy between culture and change, it is likely that culture will win and change will lose.

Implementation of change that does not consider the limits imposed by the prevailing leadership climate, organization structure, and culture may amplify the problem that triggered the need for change in the first place. In addition, the potential for subsequent problems is greater.

Strategy for Implementation

The more successful instances of change in organizations of all sizes are those that involve lower-level groups in the process of either: (1) defining the problem and alternative solutions, or (2) defining solutions after higher-level management has defined the problem. In other words, those who are expected to implement the change are involved in planning for the change. This holds true for changes ranging from the design of jobs, new technology, and quality-improvement programs, to entire reorganizations of a single company and mergers of different cultures.

This "shared approach" to implementing change is very popular and involves the joint efforts of both superiors and subordinates in the entire process. Undoubtedly it appeals to our sense of democracy and fairness. But this strategy

---

Advertising, management memos, directives, and rhetoric are a waste of time, energy, and money when the reality of what is delivered to the customer is much different than what management thinks it is.

---

can fail. Before employees participate in any change effort, consider these four questions:

1. *Do the employees want to be involved?* There have been situations where, for any number of reasons, they rejected the invitation. They may have more pressing demands, such as doing their own work. Unfortunately in many instances the employees view the invitation to participate as a subtle (but not too subtle) attempt by management to manipulate them toward a solution already predetermined. Trust is a critical element in effective management. If the leadership climate of the organization has created an atmosphere of mistrust and insincerity, most attempts to involve employees will be viewed by them in cynical terms and most likely will be resisted.

2. *Are employees willing and able to voice their ideas?* Even if they are willing, employees must have the expertise in some aspect of the analysis. The technical problems associated with computer installation or automated processes may be beyond the training of front-line personnel, yet they may have very valuable insights into the impact the change will have on their jobs and on the customer, patient, client, or student.

3. *Are managers secure in their own positions?* Insecure managers will almost surely perceive any participation by employees as a threat to their authority. They might view employee participation as a sign of weakness or as undermining their status. They must be secure enough to give credit for good ideas and to give explanations for ideas of questionable merit. In other words, the managers' personalities and leadership styles must be compatible with the shared approach to implementing change if it is to be successful.

4. *Are managers open to employees' suggestions?* If management has predetermined the solution, the participation of employees will soon be recognized for what it is. Obviously management has final responsibility for the outcome and should control the situation by specifying beforehand what latitude will be given to employees. Management may define objectives, establish constraints, or whatever, as long as employees know the rules prior to their participation.

If the answer to any of these questions is a definite *no*, then there will be a limit on effective participation by employees. In any case leadership style, formal organization, culture, and characteristics of employees are key factors constraining the entire change process.

There are many managers who have ''paid later'' for the time they saved by ignoring the importance of managing change. The most significant cost is failure itself. Also, a history of having tried and failed hurts any future attempts to change, no matter how well intentioned or well managed.

Lesson #16

*When Implementing Change,
Never Confuse Management
Desires and Policies with Actual
Employee Performance.*

Seventeen

Feelings Always Influence Feelings

"One must never excuse oneself by pointing to the soldiers."

Blaise Montluc

Several months ago a friend of mine was waiting his turn at an automatic teller machine. There was a couple in front of him who was also waiting. When it was their turn, the man asked the woman, who was his wife, for her card. She fumbled through her purse and gave it to him. He inserted the card, punched in the numbers and waited. In a few moments the card was returned. Apparently there was not enough money in the account. He cursed and tried the procedure again with the same result. He took the card out of the machine, handed it to his wife, and said, "Your bank stinks!" His wife replied, "That's not my bank, I only work

137

there." My friend thought to himself, "Boy, I sure am glad I won't be asking you for a loan tomorrow morning."

A few months later I spent a day with the president of a bank while attending a seminar. The seminar was in a far-away city, but I remember thinking after our conversation that the bank president and the woman mentioned above could easily have worked for the same bank.

It seems that the bank president was upset because of the dismal sales results the bank was achieving with a recently introduced product. We talked for a while about it and about some of the possible causes. Finally he said, "I'm sure I know the cause—my CSRs [customer service repre-sentatives] stink, and my tellers stink."

I remember thinking, "Maybe you stink." Here was, I'm sure, a reasonably intelligent individual who is probably a very good banker when it is time to make a loan or select an investment. He would no doubt stand up and take credit for any success his organization had in these areas. But take his banker hat off and put his manager/leader hat on, and the results are different. Somehow in his mind the odor and stench that permeated the entire bank somehow stopped at his door. He was the president but was not responsible for and could do little to get rid of the odor. He was very much like the woman standing at the automatic teller machine. Neither of them was responsible for what went on in their organizations. But this guy was the president. It was clear to me that there was very little leadership taking place in either organization.

Both of these incidents reminded me of a distinctly new aspect of work, especially in service businesses, the "feel-ing" or "emotional" part of the job. Karl Albrecht aptly de-scribes it as "emotional labor" in his book *At America's*

Service.[1] Emotional labor is any kind of work in which the employee's feelings are part of the job. Therefore, feelings can influence job performance in such cases. This is why I would not want to be a customer of the bank whose employee my friend encountered at the ATM machine. And it is why I wanted to tell the bank president that I was not at all surprised by what was going on in his bank. With his attitude toward the bank's employees he is fortunate the employees show up for work in the morning.

We can tell employees how to dress, how to behave, what to say, and when to smile. But there is one thing we cannot tell them, and that is how they should feel. Customer-contact jobs in particular involve a high degree of emotional labor. Sales professionals, complaint managers, lost-baggage personnel, college professors, most bank employees, flight attendants, restaurant servers, telephone operators, grammar school and secondary school teachers, police officers, nurses, physicians, and social workers are a few examples of jobs high in emotional labor—where feelings can influence performance. In fact they are often the sum and substance of the job itself.

The important point of course is that negative feelings can spill over onto the customer, passenger, student, client, or patient, thereby contaminating the quality of the service delivered. Service businesses sell human performances, and feelings influence human performance. Negative feelings can show up in employee apathy (undoubtedly what the bank president is up against); hostility toward customers; indifference toward the job, the customers, and the organization ("That's not my bank, I only

---

[1]Karl Albrecht, *At America's Service* (Homewood, Ill.: Dow Jones-Irwin, 1988), pp. 111–14.

work there."); a loss of interest in the quality of one's work; and an overall I-don't-give-a-damn attitude.

At the close of my conversation with the bank president he seemed to have resigned himself to the fact that his CSRs and tellers would always stink. The only solution he could think of was a quick-fix one, which he knew he could never implement. He seemed to be fantasizing when he said, "What I really need to do but know I never could is hire only former school teachers and flight attendants for customer-contact jobs. They love to help people and have nice personalities. And they wouldn't give me any headaches."

Managers can tell employees how to dress, shake hands, behave, smile, and what to say, but never, ever, how to feel.

This man really believed that is all he would need to do to solve his problem. Note, it required nothing from him but the exercise of his power to hire and fire. To him that was the essence of the managerial job. Management in this organization has become little more than administration. This is not only the case in many banks but in other mature service industries like utilities, hospitals, insurance companies, hotel and motel chains, and restaurant chains.

But when the quality of the service delivered, and ultimately the performance of the organization, is influenced by how employees feel, employees need more from their managers than rules, policies, procedures, and directives. I wanted very much to tell the bank president that, if he hired a dozen of Delta's best flight attendants, within six months of working in his organization they too would stink. What his employees need is more management and leadership and a lot less administration. Once again, we can tell people what we want them to do, but we can't tell them how to feel.

Lesson #17

How Your Employees Feel Is Eventually How Your Customers Will Feel.

Eighteen

Managing the "A" People

The time to repair the roof is when the sun is shining.

John F. Kennedy

I had landed late at a hub city and missed my connecting flight. There was another one in four hours, so I decided to try my luck on a commuter airline that had a flight leaving for my destination in less than an hour.

All of the check-in counters for this airline were located in one area, so I waited in line in front of a sign that listed the city of my destination. After about 10 minutes I was told that this particular flight was an earlier one that had already left and that the passengers for the flight I wanted were being checked in at another counter. After 10 to 15 minutes at that counter, the agent told me my flight check-in had been moved to another counter. I went to the new counter.

I handed my ticket to the agent, and she said, ''Sir, you should check in at the next counter.'' Now since the next counter was part of her counter and she could actually reach over and touch the computer, I said, ''Look lady, I am a Customer! This is the third line I've waited in and I'm not waiting in another one. I am a Customer! *You* take two steps to the left and check me in.''

She was a little startled, but she did what I requested. When she handed me my boarding pass, she said, ''Sir, we try not to use the 'C' word around here.''

''The 'C' word,'' I thought. So that is what I had become, ''The Big C.'' I wanted very much to tell her since we were using code letters that she was the ''A'' word, but I decided against it.

Instead, I couldn't help but think of the incredible managing-people challenge U.S. managers are facing if customers are becoming the ''C'' word in a great many businesses.

We ended Part I of the book with a kind of summary lesson on customer satisfaction. It seems appropriate to end Part II with a summary lesson on managing people. It seems that an important question at this point is, ''Are there any commonalities involved in managing people in the 'Decade of the Customer' that managers can agree on?''

During the past several years I have had the opportunity to speak with or interview hundreds of senior executives, most of whom are considered successful by their peers. The topic of managing people always comes up. There appears to be three clear commonalities about managing people that continually dominate the discussions in one way or another:

(1) Any change must begin with you.
(2) It's a different job.
(3) You can't do it alone.

CHANGE MUST BEGIN WITH YOU

Anyone who has ever gone white-water rafting knows that change is a permanent part of the environment. It is also a great metaphor for managing people in the "Decade of the Customer." Adapting to change requires organizations that are flexible and responsive. But the best managers (and rafters) understand that managing in today's environment involves more than steering the organization from a stable "blue-water" condition through a turbulent transition to another stable condition. It involves managing in constant "white water" and turbulence. One CEO summarized it well when he told me, "We are being forced to throw away the old tradition. We don't have time to move people from the bottom to the top. Today we have to go out and get managers who are ready to go."

One of the most important, although subtle, differences between effective and less effective managers is this: The best managers understand that they must begin the process of change with themselves and conclude with the people who do the work. *They never ask the people who do the work to also create change.* Throughout this book we have seen the impact on customers when the employees are the only ones in the organization who are expected to change. In such instances customers are likely to become the "C" word.

Less effective managers begin implementing change with the people who do the work. They often assume that change is for everyone but them. Belatedly, they recognize the need to change their own behavior. But the best managers seem to know that developing new strategy is an "outside-in" process, while the changes necessary to implement new strategy involve an "inside-out" process that begins with themselves.

IT'S A DIFFERENT JOB

In the days of blue water, management selection decisions in many industries ran little risk of failure because many individuals possessed the knowledge and skill to be an effective manager. This is because technical knowledge and

---

Managing today involves more than moving the organization from a stable condition through a turbulent transition into another stable condition. There are no stable conditions.

---

administrative skills, not management and leadership skills, were the primary basis for selecting managers in most industries.

In blue water, an organization can perform well as long as it has people in management positions with sound technical knowledge and some administrative capability. By administration, we mean the ability to carry out the activities required by the organization's rules, policies, and procedures.

Today's best managers are not only skilled in the technical aspects of the business and are good administrators; they also understand the critical importance of managing people as a way to influence the direction of their organization or unit. They also know that leadership is more than a repopularized word with mystical connotations. It requires competence and expertise in management as well as the technical aspects of the business.

In fact, the best managers make a very clear distinction between the technical aspects of the business and managing people and identify managing people as the area where they need the most improvement.

Finally, the best managers understand that managing people in white water requires more than administration, more than giving instructions and monitoring performance. They realize that bureaucratic management can be very dangerous in a competitive white-water environment.

YOU CAN'T DO IT ALONE

Today's effective managers have made the transition from "I the manager" to "we the management." They understand that hierarchical/bureaucratic management with secrecy at the top chokes the creativity and competitiveness needed in a white-water environment. Very little gets done where no one can make a decision without going through numerous channels and where managers spend most of their time protecting their own turf.

They also know that one person rarely has all the information or knowledge to solve a problem. Thus teams and team building are becoming increasingly essential as ways to deal with change because they bring together the expertise necessary to deal with the complex problems of a white-water environment. I remember a group of friends who just returned from a rafting trip commenting on how much more effective they were than the group in an accompanying raft because they had previously worked as a team on some other projects.

Finally, the best managers recognize that the leadership component of all managerial jobs is getting bigger and that it can no longer be the exclusive domain of the CEO. Thus, in addition to the importance of developing teams, they also appreciate the necessity of developing the management and leadership capabilities of others in the organization.

Lesson #18

*There Are New Rules
for Managers:*
1. Change Must Begin with You.
2. It's a Different Job.
3. You Can't Do It Alone.

CHECKLIST FOR PART II
Lessons from Customers about Managing People
▼

✔ Never allow an employee's work to interfere with his job.

✔ You will never treat your customers any better than you treat each other.

✔ Do what any good physician does: Separate the problems of your job from the conditions of your job, and never try to cure a condition.

✔ The most important parts of employees' contributions to the goals of your organization are being made at their discretion.

✔ Most employees want to commit to something bigger than the numbers.

✔ When implementing change, never confuse management desires and policies with actual employee performance.

✔ How your employees feel is eventually how your customers will feel.

✔ There are new rules for managers:
  1. Change must begin with you.
  2. It's a different job.
  3. You can't do it alone.

PART
III

What Customers Know about Leadership

Nineteen

There Are Some Things You Can't Give at the Office

"Leadership is action, not position."

Donald H. McGammon

I don't remember exactly what year it was in grammar
school that I had my first management experience. My
friend Richie and I had done something our teacher did not
approve of that was apparently beyond her tolerance level
for unacceptable behavior. She told us she was sending us
to the "office." As young as I was, I knew that this could
not be good.

There were a few chairs separated by a two-foot-high
wooden gate from a reception area. We were finally invited
through the gate and led into the office. I learned that the

person behind the desk was the school principal and she was the "boss" of the entire grammar school and had a very fancy office. This was my first visit to a manager's office. I never went back to this particular one and never saw the principal again. But little did I know at the time that for the rest of my life, whenever I needed to see the manager, he or she would always be in their office.

In high school I somehow got involved as the middleman for the boy in the row to my left and the one in the row to my right. I was merely passing what are now known as sexually explicit materials from one to the other when the teacher intercepted them. She didn't believe that I had my eyes closed the entire time and sent all three of us to the dean's office.

From the paneling in his office and the size of his desk, it was clear that he was far more important than any of the teachers. He was their "boss." He was the manager, and I was once again in a manager's office. I remember wondering what he did all day because he didn't teach any classes and whether he had a great collection of confiscated sexually explicit materials.

And so it has been all my life. In grocery stores, hospitals, department stores, hotels, banks, and universities, if for any reason I needed to see a manager, I have always been sent to their office where I would find them sitting behind their desk.

Once I was in a bank, and the teller told me that I would have to have a document initialed by the branch manager. She pointed to a glass-enclosed office in the corner of the branch. Apparently the manager did not want to see any employees or customers during business hours because the blinds had been drawn on all of the windows.

I knocked and entered. The branch manager was sitting behind his desk, rubbing Vaseline Intensive Care lotion on his hands. I was afraid to ask if I was interrupting anything. Although I was in a hurry, I had to wait until his hands had dried so he could grip a pen and keep the lotion from getting on my document.

Several years ago a top administrator of my university announced he was retiring. I suddenly realized that I had never met the man. I had seen his picture in the paper and on TV, but had never met my manager in person. I guess the reason was that in my time at that university I had never done anything good enough or bad enough to be invited to the office.

Then one day I was watching a baseball game on TV, and, though I had never thought about it before, I noticed the manager was standing at the foot of the dugout. While it was unfortunate that he was spitting tobacco juice all over the floor, at least he was there in full view of all employees and customers during business hours.

The same can be said for the managers of basketball and football teams. They are right there, visible to their subordinates and customers. Don Shula, Rick Pitino, Earl Weaver, Joe B. Hall, and Billy Martin were "managing by walking around" long before Peters and Waterman wrote about it, before Sam Walton began visiting his Wal-Mart stores, and before Stew Leonard mingled with the customers of his dairy store.

Imagine for a moment what baseball would be like if the teams were managed like a school, hospital, bank, or any other business for that matter, where managers remained in their office during business hours. Before the third-base coach could flash the hit-and-run sign, or signal for a bunt, he would have to go to the clubhouse office and check with the manager. When a pitcher was replaced, he would be sent to the manager's office. If there were any disagreements on balls and strikes, safe or out calls, or other disputes, the umpires would have to go the manager's office to have the rhubarb. Earl and Billy would have had to kick sand on the umpire out of view of all employees and customers.

But instead, during business hours baseball managers advise, encourage, and coach. They promote a sense of team and are visible, active supporters and advocates of their employees.

Don Shula, Rick Pitino, Earl Weaver, Joe B. Hall, and Billy Martin were "managing by walking around" long before anyone wrote about it in a management book.

And if customers have complaints, they needn't ask to see the manager. They can register their complaints with boos, along with 25,000 or more other customers. Remember, for a baseball manager, the quality of the product and his job performance get evaluated 162 times a year. For a football coach, the quality of the product and his job performance get evaluated every Sunday in front of about 100,000 customers and a TV audience in the millions. Suppose the same were true for managers in business, health care, education, and government.

Not long ago I drove a friend to pick up his car at the dealership where he had left it for servicing. As we waited for them to bring his car, I noticed a man circulating among the wells, looking under and into cars, and chatting with the technicians and mechanics. He spotted me and came over and introduced himself and told me he was the manager of the service department, as well as a former student from a decade before.

I took the opportunity to smartly remark that I thought managers were supposed to be in their office at their desks, or at least that was where I had always found them. I jokingly asked if his office was being repainted or repaneled.

He told me that he thought it was better for him to be close to where the work was being carried out—*not* in his office. Since my friend's car was made in Japan, I wasn't surprised by what he said. Unlike typical U.S. managers, whose success is measured by the size of their office, most Japanese managers have very small offices or no office at all. In fact, Nobuhiko Kawamoto, the new president of Honda, has no private office. (Could it be that this is a management lesson that the Japanese have learned from American sports?)

He asked my friend if he had ever had any problems with the service he received. He said *no.* He gave each of us his card, wished us well, and said, "Keep in touch."

I didn't think anything about his final remark until two weeks later when my friend received a call from the dealership. The caller mentioned the service manager's name and said he wanted to know whether the repairs had been done to his satisfaction, whether there were any complaints or suggestions for improvements, and how he rated the service he received.

I don't know if the service department manager learned anything while he was in my class 10 years ago, but I certainly learned something from him: There are far too many principals, deans, hospital administrators, presidents, bankers, and managers of every variety who are deskbound.

Lesson #19

Management and Leadership Are Exercised Outside, Not Inside the Office.

Twenty

Leaders Must Manage and Managers Must Lead

"We've got to be sure we don't create organizations with a CEO at the top, a computer in the middle, and lots of workers at the bottom."

Robert T. Tomasko

While they may not read the business pages or the latest business books, your customers notice that there has been a lot of "management bashing" going on lately. Numerous books and articles are saying that our nation's organizations are "overmanaged and underled" and that we must develop a leadership capability in our organizations. We see the glut of books on leadership in local bookstores. It is as if leaders and managers are two distinctly different animals and that we have bred too many of one and not enough of the other. So we must now turn our attention to breeding more of the other.

165

That is far too simplistic of an analysis. Customers see managers of hamburger franchises, airline stations, hotel front desks, and bank branches, all of whom are at the lowest managerial levels, exhibit some outstanding leadership skills on a daily basis. Some of these managers are true leaders of the people they manage.

And while such statements as "most organizations are overmanaged and underled" may sound good from the speaker's platform, they tell us little about: (1) the implications of such a statement, (2) the nature of the problem, and (3) the important relationship between management and leadership. Just making such statements accomplishes nothing.

It is these issues that we will examine here. We must first look at some differences between management and leadership and then, far more importantly, at the relationships between them.

MANAGEMENT AND EFFICIENCY

Management is a process, a discipline. Managers cope with complexity. They achieve through the management functions of planning, administration, budgeting, and control. The purpose of the discipline of management is to implement strategy and change rather than formulate them. By necessity, therefore, managers must focus their attention inward. They must be more process-oriented as they concentrate on improving existing operations. In other words, *management* is required to make sure an organization is *efficient—that it does things right. But accomplishing this task often involves leadership capabilities.*

LEADERSHIP AND EFFECTIVENESS

Leadership requires the conceptual skills to formulate a vision, create goals, build an organization structure, and create a shared sense of purpose and an environment where people want to do their best work. So while managers cope with complexity, leaders cope with change. The purpose of leadership is to formulate strategy and change rather than implement them. By necessity, therefore, leaders must focus their attention outward. They must be more results-oriented as they concentrate on developing strategy in response to change and on establishing goals. In other

It is naive to think that managers and leaders are two different animals and that we have bred too many of one and not enough of the other.

words, *leadership* is required to make sure an organization is *effective*—that it *does the right things. But accomplishing this task often involves management capabilities.*

LEADERS AS MANAGERS AND MANAGERS AS LEADERS

In most organizations managers at all levels are now being asked on a regular basis to take on more—and new—responsibilities. They are expected to be catalysts, prompting other people to change, to perform at higher levels, and to put forth the extra effort needed to improve productivity and performance. This means producing change and managing the effects of change at all levels of the organization. And it therefore requires effective leadership and management skills at all levels of the organization.

So while there are some very important differences between management and leadership, the real question is, "Do the differences make a difference?" Examine Figure 1. It illustrates some possible combinations of management and leadership.

1. *Failure.* It is easy to see that an organization with no capacity for management or leadership must eventually fail. It must fail because it is both ineffective as well as inefficient. It has no strategy or vision and no capability to implement. When you do the wrong things and then implement them poorly, you must fail. (Unfortunately, we must omit many of our tax-supported bureaucracies from this generalization. In their case we find that a lack of strategy and vision, inability to implement, and inefficient operations are not a threat to survival.)

Figure 1   The Results of Various Capacities for Management and Leadership

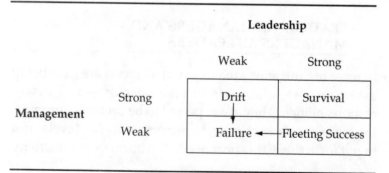

2. *Fleeting Success.* An organization with a strong leadership capability but a weak management capability has lots of visionaries, strategists, and planners on the payroll but no capacity to implement consistently. You can often get away with doing the right things poorly for a while, but in the long run a lack of management capacity may lead to failure because of inefficient operations, overstaffing, waste, fiscal losses, dissatisfied customers, and no repeat business. The organization is effective but inefficient. Any successes in strategy cannot be sustained.

This type of situation often occurs when the price or demand for a product is so high that it hides any deficiencies in management—at least for a while. But sooner or later, the inability to implement and inefficient operations bring down the organization. It must either acquire managerial skills or, as in the case of some high-tech companies (e.g., Apple, Atari), motels, book publishers, and fast-food chains, sell the business to someone who has these skills if any success is to be sustained.

Some airlines and banks and savings and loans were in this quadrant prior to the deregulation of their industries, but did not know it. You are probably thinking at this point, "How is it possible for a regulated business to be strong in leadership and weak in management when a regulated business requires no leadership skills, only some management capability, to be successful?"

It is possible because in reality it was the regulators who performed the leadership function in the airline and banking industries prior to deregulation. They were actually absentee leadership who legislated strategy. After deregulation, many of these airlines and financial institutions found that, while they had never needed to develop a capacity for leadership, they unfortunately had no capacity for management either. Most such airlines and financial institutions have either already failed or been acquired.

3. *Drift*. How about an organization with strong management skills but no capacity for leadership? Those who argue that most organizations are overmanaged and underled would place them in this quadrant. An organization with lots of managers and no leadership will almost certainly find itself drifting. A drifting organization continually misses major market opportunities, trails and imitates the competition, is unable to make needed changes, and has low employee morale because of the lack of a clear vision, unifying goals, and a shared sense of purpose. These are the definite symptoms of a drifting organization.

Organizations in this quadrant often continue to define themselves in the terms and conditions under which they were born, not under which they must now operate. As a result, they are very efficient but ineffective. Many hospitals and financial institutions are in my opinion drifting organizations. An organization doing with great efficiency that which it should not be doing is in great need of leadership.

Drifting organizations need a renewed search for purpose, a new vision. If the needed leadership is not forthcoming, sooner or later they will manage themselves into the ground, like many hospitals, or become good takeover targets because of their efficient operations, like many banks.

4. *Survival.* Effective leadership and management spell survival no matter what the organization does. Management has a clear vision, strategy, and shared sense of purpose that energizes employees. Their strong management skills ensure efficient operations and sound implementation. They continually do the right things and do them well. The results are productivity, efficiency, adaptiveness, developed and satisfied employees, and satisfied customers. These results equal survival, the ultimate indicator of effective management and leadership.

DIFFERENT MANAGERIAL CAPABILITIES

Leaders and managers are not different people, but leadership and management are two different tasks or functions that must be performed well if an organization is to survive. They are capabilities that must exist to some extent in all managers.

The following are additional conclusions of this essay:

1. Management and leadership capabilities are two distinctly different dimensions of effective organizational performance. This means that an organization can be strong in one and weak in the other. It also means that we cannot make up for a void in one by substituting more of the other.

2. It is possible for an organization to lack both a management and leadership capacity.

3. Different and clearly identifiable symptoms arise when an organization is strong in one and weak in the other (see above examples).

4. Leadership is the foundation for all success; management is a necessary condition for survival and profitability in order to remain successful. This simply means that every new successful business excels in the skills of leadership prior to the development of a management capability that ensures long-term survival.

5. At various stages of an organization's or industry's evolution one may be more important than the other.

Lesson #20

Management and Leadership Must Be Thought of as Different Tasks or Functions, Not as Different People, Because the Leadership Component of Most Managerial Jobs Has Expanded.

Twenty-One

Leaders Have Size, Speed, Quickness, Good Hands, and the Ability to See the Whole Floor

"And that's the way it is."

Walter Cronkite

To customers, average managers' egos and self-esteem have to be sturdy because it seems that almost everyday managers are being told what they should do and be in order to be effective. They read and listen to the accounts of the accomplishments of successful business leaders and the newest entrepreneurs, and hear about their vision, creativity, and ability to energize, inspire, and motivate others toward the achievement of great things. However, a lot of what managers hear and read may be "noninformation," not "misinformation."

175

What is noninformation? According to Professor Leonard R. Sayles of Columbia University, noninformation is information that is very appealing and appears very realistic and practical. Unfortunately, the information is useless. Now where is all of this information delivered? According to Professor Sayles, a great many management consultants, seminars, and speeches deliver noninformation. He provides the following examples:

- Leadership skills should be bolstered by clear communications.
- Hire people with the potential to move to more responsible positions.

Recently I attended a seminar. Here is some of the advice I left with:

- Effective leaders are demanding but empathetic.
- Quality service is meeting customer expectations, whatever they are.
- The best CEOs surround themselves with people who complement their weaknesses.
- Good leaders have the visionary ability to see the big picture.
- Effective managers must have the ability to motivate.
- Effective CEOs are very competitive.

So what is wrong with this kind of advice? It sounds useful, valid, and makes a great deal of sense. The problem is that it doesn't contain any useful information.

Like many customers I like to read and listen to opinions on the traits and characteristics of successful leaders and entrepreneurs. Customers also like to listen to a basketball coach tell the booster club that a leader on the basketball court has size, speed, quickness, good hands, and the ability to see the whole floor (in management, the latter is known as visionary skills) as he or she orchestrates the team to victory.

Talking about the characteristics of successful business leaders and basketball team leaders is fun. Even though we have heard it many times before, and we can't possibly disagree with anything that is being said, it still makes us feel good and often inspires us. We usually end up concluding that we also have many of their same characteristics. For example, I think I'm empathetic, reasonably competitive, and a good communicator.

And that is the point. Telling a manager that he or she must become a visionary and strategist, an energizer and motivator of people, and a great communicator, and that he or she must surround themselves with good people is no different than my high school basketball coach telling our gym class that he was looking for kids with size, speed, quickness, and good hands (whatever they are) to try out for the basketball team. Both situations involve noninformation, although the information is certainly valid, practical, down-to-earth advice. You certainly cannot disagree with any of it, but in both cases the information isn't very useful.

As Professor Sayles says, everyone talks about good leadership being important—but little is done about it. Knowing the word itself and repeating it with some frequency—"leadership, leadership, leadership"—doesn't do much good.

Good intentions aren't very useful in business, in basketball, or in life. What does help, however, is to know "how" to do these things and what the barriers to implementation are.

I can remember asking my friend Larry in high school, "How do I know if I have size, speed, quickness, good hands, and the ability to see the whole floor?" I knew I could play the piano better than anyone on the basketball team but I didn't know if that meant I had good hands. I also knew that, if I stood at one end of the gym, I could see the whole basketball floor. I also remember asking Larry, "If I don't have size, speed, quickness, and good hands, how do I get some?"

While the information isn't very useful, hearing and reading about the traits and characteristics of successful CEOs, sports figures, and entrepreneurs are always fun.

Managers desiring to improve their management and leadership skills should ask the same question about visionary skills, communication and motivation skills, and choosing the right people with whom to surround themselves. Otherwise such information, however valid, will remain forever as noninformation.

So the problem is really not with all the noninformation. The problem is what to do next. What does a manager do who really wants to improve his or her management and leadership skills, and who really wants to do more than get inspired by hearing and reading about what successful leaders and managers do and have? There are certainly thousands of ideas, concepts, programs, seminars, books, methods, and audio and video programs that propose to make you a better manager and leader.

Consider the following four criteria before you sign up for a Rambo survival camp, jump in the pool with the sharks, walk over hot coals, or study under Attila the Hun. They can also be useful in evaluating less ambitious pursuits such as short courses or seminars.

1. *Does it provide a quick fix?* There is no fun and easy way to become an effective manager and leader. Many such ways have been proposed, and the fact that many of them outsell the collected works of Peter Drucker is testimony to the preference for the fun and easy over the hard and difficult. But a real commitment to professional and self-development usually occurs after the quick fix has been rejected.

2. *Are the benefits renewable and repeatable?* Whatever it is supposed to do for you, it should do it more than once. In other words, you should be able to define the benefit and it should be renewable and repeatable. You should receive the benefit more than once.

If the only benefit you get is a jolt of good feelings, then what you may be getting is inspiration, the equivalent of a good locker room talk from your high school coach. Now there is nothing wrong with inspiration, and we can all use some of it. But it's a long road from inspiration to implementation.

3. *Can you teach it to others?* You should be able to teach whatever benefit you receive to others and/or modify

it to suit your organization. For example, a friend of mine taught me two time-management principles he had learned from an audio program he had purchased and I have never stopped thanking him. Thus, the benefits he received from the program are renewable and repeatable (we use them everyday), *and* he was able to teach them to others.

4. *Are the results measurable*? Will you be a more effective communicator, planner, supervisor, trainer, or time manager? Will it improve your thinking or creativity? Will it produce measurable results?

These four criteria will assist in implementing good intentions and inspirations. As for my attempts at acquiring size, speed, quickness, and good hands, I gave up when I heard the coach tell his assistant, ''Donnelly is small but he's slow.'' To this day I have been unable to find out whether my hands are good.

Lesson #21

Being Told What You Need to Do and Be Is One Thing; Becoming It Is Another Thing Entirely.

Twenty-Two

Technology Gives but It Also Takes Away

"Understand the technology you work for so well that you control it instead of letting it control you."

George W. Dudley

Most of us do not know Johannes Faust but are very familiar with his legacy. Faust was a well-known magician and adventurer who lived in Germany in the 1500s. Strange legends and weird tales were told about him in his lifetime, and after his death there was attached to his name much ancient and medieval material that had to do with sorcery, the devil, and astrology.

Stories, ballads, dramas, operas, and epics have been written about the "Faust theme." The plots were based on a learned, pious, and well-intentioned man who sold his soul to the devil in return for superhuman powers. This was usually for a period of 24 years, after which the devil dragged Faust to hell. Why should we be interested in Johannes Faust? Because many managers may be unknowingly striking a "Faustian bargain" in their relationship with technology today.

History has illustrated that technology never gives us anything without taking something else away. So before we so willingly take from technology we should ask, "What are we going to have to give up in order to receive the benefits?" because there is always a price. The problem of course is that it is often impossible to estimate what the price will be because in most cases technology will have totally unpredictable impacts that cannot be foreseen at the time.

For example, if in 1947 we as customers were asked to vote on whether we wanted the unforeseen impacts of television, and if we knew then what we know now, I suspect many of us would have voted *no*! But back then there was no way we could have known or predicted the social costs of television.

As is still the case today we would have been more concerned with what the new technology was going to do for us, not what it would also undo for us. It would have been a better radio, and we would not have had to go out and wait in line at the movies to see pictures and voices. The decision would have been an easy one. We would have seen only the benefits. Television combined the best of both radio and the movies (sound and pictures) and did away with the worst of each (no pictures and waiting in line in bad weather). We couldn't lose. At the very worst television would have replaced radio and hurt movie ticket sales.

Now with the benefit of hindsight let's look at what television undid for us. Among other things it changed (and most

I believe would agree not for the better) how we educate, how we entertain, how we elect our leaders, and how we worship. Some say it has also done away with childhood in America.[1] Today's children may be the first generation in the history of the world that are privy to adult information before they are able to read. They have watched us wage war, assassinate leaders, spill oil, and known which sports or TV personality was the latest to die a tragic drug death. They have watched the Challenger disaster and Miss America resign her crown, and may have watched the rear of Gary Hart's friend's townhouse to see who came out—all on the 6 o'clock news. *Technology gives but it also takes away.*

At this point let me assure you that I have nothing at all against television. I have enjoyed the benefits of the greatest technological breakthrough in the history of humankind all my life. But it is a wonderful example of the point I wish to make in this essay.

When television was introduced on a wide scale in the late 1940s, the dating (I think it was called courting in those days) center of America was the front porch or more often the living room. Courting couples would do whatever courting couples did in those days on the porch or in the living room while the rest of the family slept upstairs.

In 1949 Dad decided to buy the family a television so they could watch Milton Berle, never really giving much thought as to where he would put it when it was delivered. When it arrived, where did they put it? The only logical place was the living room. That evening, when the courting couple came home, where were Mom, Dad, and little

---

[1]Neil Postman, *Conscientious Objections: Stirring Up Trouble about Language, Technology, and Education* (New York: Alfred A. Knopf, 1988), pp. 147–61. This essay was inspired by Postman's work.

brothers and sisters? You guessed it, in the living room watching television. *Technology gives but it also takes away.*

Thus television also irrevocably changed the social and dating habits of Americans when it pushed the dating couple out of the house and into the car. By the mid-1950s, the automobile was the dating center of America. Also, as an indirect result of television, drive-in movies and restaurants sprouted up all across the country so the courting couple would have some place to go.

Then in 1956 space travel began to find its way into the news, and in 1957 the Russians launched Sputnik, the first space satellite. A technological marvel with its own impacts, it brought America into the space race. Everyone wanted to go to engineering school, and the new space industry convinced us we had to catch the Russians. Rockets and spaceships were everywhere. The most popular movies and television shows featured space travel. But more important to our discussion here is that the first bucket seats in automobiles were introduced in 1956.

They were to make us feel in tune with the times. They were to give us the feeling of spaceships, cockpits, and rockets. The cars of the day also had fins like a rocket. Unfortunately bucket seats were not widely ordered by the age group that had been pushed out of the living room and into the car by television. Apparently, dating couples could not do whatever dating couples did in 1956 in automobiles with bucket seats. Thus television also indirectly impacted the design of automobiles because within a short time the bench seat (with slight buckets) returned as an available option for car buyers.

Finally, in today's home we have constructed a special temple for the television. It is a room that never before existed and is usually called the family room although some appropriately call it the TV room. Of course we still have the living room, but no one is allowed in there anymore. It has become an obsolete room that we can't quite figure out what to do with. I have been in homes where a gate blocks the entrance to the living room and the furniture is covered with bed sheets. How were we to know in 1949 that television would ultimately influence the design of our homes?

The point of all of this for today's manager should be clear. In our haste to reap the benefits of technology, we must always stop to ask what some of the costs are likely to be. Because, as the well-intentioned man of every Faustian

---

The total price of technology is often impossible to estimate because its real impact cannot be foreseen at the time. Television turned out to be a great deal more than a better radio.

---

theme finds out, there is a price to pay for the superhuman powers he receives. And we may not be willing to pay the price if we take the time to consider what it might be. As a manager, at the very least we should attempt to consider what the negative impacts on our business and customers might be.

For example, although no one seems to know if it is going to help, it is still widely accepted that every MBA (actually every third grader) must have a personal computer. The result has been that we have continued to thwart their development of writing and oral communication skills. We have put them in front of a screen when many have trouble stringing two literate sentences together. But when they have finished, they can do a great spread-sheet analysis.

What is the biggest complaint that top managers and corporate recruiters have about today's business school graduates? We should not be surprised to find out that it is their inability to communicate orally, and in writing. *Technology gives but it also takes away.*

Finally, there are many financial institutions that have rushed to move their retail customers to machines and electronic transfers in order to reap the benefits of technology. The result? They have found themselves forced in one way or another into the telemarketing and direct mail businesses in order to talk with their retail customers. *Technology gives but it also takes away.*

Lesson #22

*Ask Not Only What Technology
Will Do for You; Ask Also What it
Will Undo for You.*

Twenty-Three

Sometimes Nothing Changes but the Leaves on the Trees

"The art of progress is to preserve order amid change and to preserve change amid order."

Alfred North Whitehead

N ot long ago I was cleaning out my personal library of old books and papers in order to make room for newer material. In a way it's like cleaning out your grandmother's attic. You never get very far because you find yourself sitting in the middle of the floor looking at old yearbooks and wedding albums. And you hardly throw anything away because you can't decide what to keep and what to discard.

That is exactly what happened as I attempted to clean out my office. But I gained a great deal from the experience. I found published proceedings from several different industry conventions that took place in the late 1960s and early 1970s. In those days, the speeches and presentations at industry meetings were often bound and sold as a volume by the trade association sponsoring the meeting. Today, of course, they are recorded and sold on cassettes in our age of high tech. There were also articles and news stories from the same era.

Although hardly anything was thrown away, the afternoon was not wasted. It was very enlightening to review these materials. They told me how far we haven't come.

There was a 1965 article scolding top managers for not encouraging ethical behavior among subordinate managers. It told the story of a fraud trial and of a company that sold a worthless diet pill to the consumer via radio and television for seven years. The need for organizations to change their behavior to more ethical conduct was stressed throughout the article.

In a 1969 volume there was a speech by a consumer products executive encouraging his peers to become more customer-oriented in their product development efforts. In 1971 at a meeting of retailers there was a presentation emphasizing the necessity to improve service to customers and how customer service could become a competitive variable that could differentiate one store from another. Finally there was a series of 1972 presentations given at a banking convention that exhorted banks to become "sales organizations" and gave advice on how banks needed to change and become more sales-oriented.

It occurred to me in a very distressing way that, if I changed a few phrases, "customer-oriented" to "market driven," "service to customers" to "service quality," and "sales organizations" to "sales cultures," and left the crime the same in the ethics article and just changed the name of the company to any number of ones currently in the daily press, all of the presentations could have been given at any major convention in any industry today. The only thing that has changed is that we listen to them now when we jog or on our way to work in our car. Back then we had to read them.

CHANGE HAS ALWAYS BEEN THE SOLUTION

The theme then and now seems to be that the solution to our problems is that organizations and managers must change. They must change to become more ethical or market driven, or to deliver higher-quality service, and so on. We always have and we continue to view change as the solution.

As I sat on the floor of my office surrounded by the brown-around-the-edges speeches from the 1960s and 1970s, I couldn't help but think that, while some progress has hopefully been made in service and product quality, attention to customer needs, and ethical behavior, the people that make these speeches and presentations before industry groups are either decades ahead of everyone else, talking to themselves, or preaching to the converted, or we need to focus our energies in another direction.

I am convinced it is the latter. I propose that *changing organizations is not the solution, it is the problem.* Managing change is the solution, and it is here that we should focus our energies.

WHEN CHANGE BECOMES THE PROBLEM

How do you get organizations to change? There are only three ways, and two of them have apparently not worked very well. One extreme is the application of power; the other extreme is the application of reason. Midway between these two extremes is an approach that relies on reeducation.

Using power implies the use of coercion. Management can use its power to coerce everyone else to change in the direction it desires. Management can implement its power through its control over rewards and sanctions. It gets to make the rules that determine the conditions of employment, including promotion and advancement.

But except in a crisis, when the very existence of the organization is at stake, power has not been successful in bringing about the changes needed in most organizations. Power cannot make people ethical, develop market-driven products and services, or give their all for customer service.

Reason alone has not been sufficient to bring about change in organizations either. The fact that we are saying basically the same things at industry meetings that we were

---

There are only three ways to get organizations to change, and it is becoming more and more apparent that in most cases two of them do not work.

---

saying 20 years ago is evidence that the application of reason has not brought about change in most organizations. Despite all the articles, exhortations, and speeches, reason has not prevailed.

So if we agree that employees won't change just because someone tells them to—power—or asks them to—reason—then it seems that the middle ground is the only approach left. Once we accept that changing organizations is not the solution but the problem, we can focus attention on strategies for producing and managing change. What we need is a formal approach to reeducation and implementing the process of change.

MANAGING CHANGE THROUGH ORGANIZATIONAL DEVELOPMENT

There is a management technique known as organizational development that has an excellent record of success in helping organizations adapt to change. Organizational development is a planned, managed, systematic process to change the culture, systems, and behavior of an organization. Its purpose is to change attitudes and values of employees, modify behavior, and induce change in organizational structure and policies. It is a formal approach to reeducation and managing that changes the way people think, behave, and act.

However, before a technique such as organizational development has any chance of bringing about successful change in any organization, two things must occur:

1. Management must recognize that the inability to change is a problem for the organization and that the use of power and reason have not brought about the needed changes.

2. Management must face the issue of who will facilitate the change, and who will be the catalyst or champion for change, the "change agent."

This issue is an important one. Are champions of change necessary for change to take place? It is difficult to imagine a successful change taking place in an organization without someone playing the role of change agent.

But who? Existing managers? New managers? Or someone hired specifically for the purpose? Depending on the situation, any of these three can orchestrate the organizational development process. The critical point is that the

role of the change agent or champion is absolutely necessary if permanent change is to occur.

The role of the change agent is to bring a different perspective and to serve as a challenge to the status quo. A definite
internal change agent is a recently appointed CEO of an organization that has a record of poor performance. Usually this
individual takes the job with the expectation that major
change is necessary. The ways that successful internal change
agents such as W. Michael Blumenthal of Burroughs Corporation, Jack Welch of General Electric Corporation, and Lee
Iacocca of Chrysler Corporation have accomplished organizational change have become widely known in recent years.

An external change agent could be an organizational development consultant, a training organization, or a change
specialist. In fact there are currently several firms specializing as organizational development and change management consultants. Obviously in the case of external change
agents the success of any change program will rest heavily
on the quality and workability of the relationship between
them and the key decision makers in the organization.

Some organizations have successfully used a combina-
tion external-internal change team, an approach that attempts to use the resources and knowledge of both groups.
It involves designating an individual or group in the organization to work with the external change agent to spearhead
the change effort. In fact, many change consultants demand an internal team.

Each of the three approaches to bringing about change
can and have worked. But none will work without the visible support of top management.

So there are ways to bring about organizational change,
whether it is to improve service quality or to facilitate a mer-
ger. But first we must admit that our inability to change is a
problem that must be solved.

Lesson #23

Changing Your Organization Is Not the Solution—It's the Problem. Managing the Process of Change Is the Solution.

Twenty-Four

Management and Leadership Do Make a Difference

"Do you have any junior leaders in your organization? Reward them by sending them to work with your best people and they will reward you with more leaders."

Jack Falvey

T he experiences that have been detailed throughout this book should leave no doubt whatsoever that from the customer's point of view there is a great need to improve the management and leadership skills in our nation's businesses, governmental agencies, educational institutions, and health-care organizations.

So it should not be a surprise that the question I am asked the most as an educator and a customer is: "Do I have leadership capacity?" It is asked by undergraduate students, graduate students, and professional development students. Somehow everyone seems to know how

199

much our nation needs to develop a greater competence in leadership. Practicing managers also ask it, but they want to know what they should look for when promoting from within or when selecting prospective employees.

But how does someone know whether he or she has the potential to contribute to this growing and much needed leadership capacity? This is a question that psychologists and management scholars have been trying to answer for years. I will not pretend that I have the answer, but I will suggest four questions that I have used successfully with students and managers for years. If you want to assess your potential as a leader, begin by examining the following:

1. Are you more comfortable working in a process-oriented culture or a results-oriented culture?

2. Do you have a low or high tolerance for ambiguity?

3. Do you depend more on systems or on people and ideas?

4. Do you view change as a transitional state or a permanent state?

These questions focus on four areas of management capability that will be critical in this decade. Honestly answering them will give you a good idea of how ready you are for a leadership role.

PROCESS OR RESULTS?

In a process-oriented culture *how* something is done is far more important than *what* is done.

In process-oriented organizations people are rewarded for what they do rather than what they accomplish—for *efforts* rather than *results*. Such is the case in most governmental bureaucracies, educational institutions, school systems, healthcare organizations, and semiregulated industries. In such organizations managers focus their attention inward, on policing and enforcing the efforts of employees.

A results-oriented culture focuses on the achievement of objectives. Managers in such organizations focus their attention outward, concentrating on the development of strategy in response to change. Such should be the case in traditional market-driven and newly deregulated industries. Employees are rewarded for *results*, not for *efforts*. Compensation systems reflect accomplishment, not authority.

Potential leaders will be more comfortable working in a results-oriented culture.

> *One of the most important questions a manager can ever ask of himself or herself is: "Do I have leadership capacity?*

LOW OR HIGH TOLERANCE FOR AMBIGUITY?

People who are more content working in process-oriented cultures usually have what psychologists describe as a low tolerance for ambiguity. They are uncomfortable with loose ends and seek clarity and closure in everything they do.

They concentrate on keeping current activities in order. When planning, they think in short time spans.

To some extent we all have a need for clarity and closure. Marketers capitalize on this tendency when they force us to complete an advertising slogan, jingle, phrase, or word on a billboard.

Taken to extremes, however, the tendency can make managers think no further than the next quarter or, at best, to think in fiscal or calendar year increments of time. They will focus on the achievement of short-term goals and objectives.

But we know that leaders must have vision and long-term goals. In other words, leaders must be strategic thinkers. All successful strategic thinkers have a high tolerance for ambiguity. They are comfortable with the fact that clarity and closure are never possible in a competitive world. As a result, they are capable of thinking in longer time spans and of seeing the forest instead of the trees.

There is no doubt that results-oriented cultures require strategic thinkers. Potential leaders, therefore, will have a high tolerance for ambiguity.

SYSTEMS OR PEOPLE AND IDEAS?

Most managers lean either toward a dependence on systems or a dependence on people and ideas. Managers with a high dependence on systems place top priority on organization, coordination, and tight controls over resources, systems, and processes.

It should not be a surprise that these managers are comfortable in process-oriented cultures. They rely heavily on accounting and financial control systems and on maximizing results from existing functions and systems. They issue directives to employees and monitor their performance.

Managers who depend highly on people and ideas are more likely to communicate the purpose of doing things. In other words, *why* we are doing something (a shared sense of purpose) rather than just *what* to do. These managers stress relationships, corporate values, and seek individual commitment—the emotional aspects of the organization.

In a process-oriented culture, commitment and creativity can be ignored. It is nice if they are present, but if they are not it doesn't really matter because they make little difference. What matters is if people do their job. In a results-oriented culture, these intangibles are vital if the organization is to survive and prosper.

Results-oriented cultures, therefore, require good people and good ideas. Potential leaders, therefore, will depend on people and ideas.

CHANGE AS TRANSITIONAL OR PERMANENT?

How managers view change is critical to how they will deal with it. If managers see change as a transitional state, their goal becomes adapting or adjusting to the change in order to get things back to the way they were before the change occurred. Change is just something to be lived through.

Process-oriented cultures are especially likely to have managers who view change as a temporary interruption. For example, there are still managers in the deregulated world of banking from whom we hear the cry to "get back to basics." I don't know what that means, but I think it means "I wish we could put everything back the way it was before deregulation."

Managers in results-oriented cultures understand that the change we are involved in is a permanent condition. Not only that, but these managers also seek to produce change. They are not satisfied with the status quo or with what they or their predecessors have achieved. They want to move their organization or unit in new directions. They are more entrepreneurial and understand that if management doesn't support change no change will occur.

Potential leaders, therefore, will view change as a permanent condition.

In conclusion, results-oriented cultures require leaders where process-oriented cultures can survive without a great leadership capacity. So results-oriented cultures obviously require managers who are comfortable with working in such climates. And to manage successfully in such a climate requires a high tolerance for ambiguity, a dependence on people and ideas, and a view of change as a permanent condition. If you gave those answers to the four questions, you have a capacity for leadership.

Lesson #24

Leaders Prefer to Work in Results-Oriented Cultures, Have a High Tolerance for Ambiguity, Depend on People and Ideas, and View Change as a Permanent Condition.

Twenty-Five

The Game Is Never Over

"The lion and the lamb may lie down together, but the lamb won't get much sleep."

Woody Allen

I t is enjoyable to watch a sporting event on TV when all the players are shouting, "We're number one!" holding up one finger for the TV cameras, and the cheerleaders and fans are in a frenzy because their team is number one.

At the beginning of each season or at the start of a tournament, every participating coach states that his or her team's goal is to win it all, to be number one. That's what coaches are supposed to say, that's what fans want to hear, and that's the goal in sports. Coaches don't figure out strategies to be number four.

And that's what often happens in business. It is impossible to imagine a CEO standing before a group of

207

customers, stockholders, or employees saying, ''Our goal is to come in fourth in sales volume next year,'' and then have everyone stand up and cheer, ''We're number four! We're number four!''

It must be a carryover from our obsession with sports. We are always supposed to be number one. But there is one important difference between sports and business. In sports, when the season or the tournament ends, you start all over again next year. In business the game is never over until somebody loses. You may be winning at a particular time, but you can never win because the game is never over. If this were the case in sports, a coach's goals and strategies would almost certainly change.

So in business, being a clearly underdog firm but having the goal of being number one, can be disastrous because it may divert the organization from doing what it does best and remaining a very profitable number four in its quest to say ''We're number one!'' Simply stated, the firm may behave as if it has the possibility to be number One, when in reality it has absolutely no chance.

The point, of course, is that while it may not be good in sports to be a perennial number four, in business it can be a very nice situation. What it takes is a clearly defined strategy and an understanding of what the organization is good at and not good at. So, unlike coaches, some managers should be trying to figure out how to be number four. They and their customers would benefit.

For an underdog firm to be really successful, it must in most cases develop a truly differentiating strategy. This strategy must be designed to build some kind of competitive advantage in some area. An underdog firm will never achieve any real degree of sustained success by imitating larger competitors or solely competing on price.

Competing as an underdog may not be easy, but the following are some alternatives to being controlled by the competition.[1]

1. *Look for vacant niches.* This involves searching out profitable areas of the market, or undefined weak points or unprotected flanks that larger companies are not catering to, are ignoring, or are not equipped to serve. Obviously the niche must be large enough to be profitable, have potential for growth, and be well suited to the company's strengths. It may involve specific market segments such as smaller companies, a particular industry, or a particular demographic segment of consumers.

2. *Specialize.* Some firms are succeeding by competing only in carefully chosen market segments with a limited product line rather than trying to compete for all customers with a complete product line and being forced to attack the dominant firms head-on with price cuts and/or large promotional expenses.

There are many success stories recently in the banking industry where banks have remained small, specializing very narrowly, emphasizing marketing, and abandoning most parts of other markets.

3. *Improve on the competition.* With the right strengths and capabilities, an underdog firm may succeed by actually improving on the product of a larger firm. Many consumer product firms have succeeded by not being a pioneering firm, but by waiting until a new product

---

[1]For more detailed discussions see James H. Donnelly, Jr., Leonard L. Berry, and Thomas W. Thompson, *Marketing Financial Services: A Strategic Vision* (Homewood, Ill.: Dow Jones–Irwin, 1985), chap. 2; and Philip Kotler, *Marketing Management*, 7th ed. (Englewood Cliffs, N.J.: Prentice-Hall, 1991), chap. 14.

appears to be a sure bet and then entering the market with a better version.

The reasoning here is that the second or third bite of a big apple can be just as juicy as, or more so than, the first. This strategy will usually involve working closely with customers in order to find the area where product improvements will make a difference.

4. *Be a smart follower.* Done consciously, it may be wise in some cases to be content to follow rather than challenge the market. This would involve carefully monitoring market share, allowing absolutely no slippage,

---

Sports metaphors are very popular in business. But there is one important difference between sports and business. In sports the season or tournament ends and you begin again next year. In business the game is never over until somebody loses.

---

and avoiding confrontations with larger organizations by not attempting to take away their customers and increase market share. This strategy requires strong top management and an internal profit emphasis rather than a market share emphasis.

5. *Focus all your competitive strength on smaller competitors.* By following this strategy, any gains in market share would be accomplished at the expense of smaller competitors. It involves identifying the weaknesses of your smaller competitors and targeting all of your competitive strength at those weaknesses.

There are also some strategies I believe underdogs should avoid. Under the stress of competition managers in underdog firms, as a result of frustration, desperation, poor advice, or poor analysis, may be attracted to a risky strategy with little chance for success. I believe the following are high-risk/low-potential strategies:

1. *Imitation.* When you try to imitate what a larger and more dominant competitor is doing, you are trying to beat a stronger opponent at its own game. It rarely achieves any meaningful results. More importantly though, imitation enables management to ignore the development of the organization's own unique strategy and direction. And *a firm without a distinct position in the minds of potential customers will always be an alternative firm to those customers.*

2. *Head-to-head competition.* For whatever reason, perhaps because of our obsession with being number one in sports, there is often an urge in some managers to seek greater market penetration by attacking the competition head-on with price cuts and lots of promotion.

For an underdog, this strategy has a big weakness— it forces retaliation and an expensive battle for market share, which no one wins, including the instigator.

3. *Halfway efforts.* When new market segments emerge or new product opportunities present themselves, it is usually best to either get in or stay out. For some reason, some underdog firms try to do both at the same time. For example, I am familiar with some firms that over the years have had products "available," but instructed personnel not to offer them unless the customer was ready to walk out the door.

I refer to these products as "mystery products." A business where management has a consciously formulated strategy does not have such products. These and similar halfway efforts seldom result in anything except an inadequate commitment by the organization, a frustrated staff, and confused customers.

4. *Duplicating a success.* When you have introduced a successful new product or created a winning advertising campaign, the temptation is to repeat the success by repeating the strategy. Trying to duplicate a success rarely works because market conditions change and/or the success requirements of the new strategy are different.

5. *Sparring matches.* Often two underdogs of the same size will enter a contest for increased market share. Lately it seems to be happening when two firms move into a new geographic market (either domestic or international) at about the same time. As one increases advertising, cuts prices, and introduces new products, the other is forced to follow for defensive reasons.

The result is a cost-increasing standoff. About the only thing these skirmishes ever really accomplish is increased costs for everyone. Customers and the advertising media may benefit, but rarely do such sparring matches ever produce any substantial changes in market share. And the dominant competitor always enjoys the show.

In today's competitive battleground, many underdog organizations are finding it tough to make sizable, as well as profitable, gains in market share. Many would probably settle for just not losing any. But as we have seen, unlike in sports, being number four is OK so long as it is done consciously, with a truly differentiating strategy designed to develop an identifiable competitive advantage in some area.

Lesson #25

If You Are an Underdog:
- *Only Compete in Market Segments where You Have or Can Develop Strengths.*
- *Avoid Head-to-Head Competition with Dominant Competitors.*
- *Emphasize Profits rather than Volume.*
- *Focus on Specialization rather than Diversification.*

CHECKLIST FOR PART III
Lessons from Customers about Leadership

▼

✔ Management and leadership are exercised outside, not inside the office.

✔ Management and leadership must be thought of as different tasks or functions, not as different people, because the leadership component of most managerial jobs has expanded.

✔ Being told what you need to do and be is one thing, becoming it is another thing entirely.

✔ Ask not only what technology will do for you, ask also what it will undo for you.

✔ Changing your organization is not the solution, it's the problem. Managing the process of change is the solution.

✔ Leaders prefer to work in results-oriented cultures, have a high tolerance for ambiguity, depend on people and ideas, and view change as a permanent condition.

✔ If you are an underdog:
   (1) Only compete in market segments where you have or can develop strengths.
   (2) Avoid head-to-head competition with dominant competitors.
   (3) Emphasize profits rather than volume.
   (4) Focus on specialization rather than diversification.

OTHER BUSINESS ONE IRWIN TITLES OF INTEREST TO YOU:

SECOND TO NONE
How Our Smartest Companies Put People First
Charles Garfield

New from Charles Garfield, whose ongoing study of high achievers was the basis for his 1986 *Time* magazine best-seller, *Peak Performers: The New Heroes of American Business.* Dr. Garfield reveals how our smartest companies are thriving in the midst of intense competition. He examines how innovative teamwork and partnership strategies will help any organization achieve peak performance in the 1990s and beyond.

ISBN: 1-55623-360-4 $22.95

THE DOMINO EFFECT
How to Grow Sales, Profits, and Market Share through Super Vision
Donald J. Vlcek, Jr., and Jeffrey P. Davidson

A behind-the-scenes look at Domino's Pizza Inc.'s meteoric rise. Vlcek and Davidson show how virtually any company can provide products and services to improve end-user satisfaction.

ISBN: 1-55623-602-6 $24.95

REBUILDING AMERICA'S WORKFORCE
Business Strategies to Close the Competitive Gap
William H. Kolberg and Foster C. Smith

Foreword by John D. Ong, Chief Executive Officer, the BF Goodrich Company. Revealing interviews with resourceful managers and case studies from progressive companies like Motorola and IBM show how improved employee performance can become a reality.

ISBN: 1-55623-622-0 $24.95

WORK IS NOT A FOUR LETTER WORD
Improving the Quality of Your Work Life
Stephen Strasser and John Sena

Minimize or eliminate the five negative emotions that prevent you from achieving success, fulfillment, and happiness in the workplace. By offering psychological exercises, question and answer sections, and relevant case studies, the authors show you how to constructively deal with work-related problems and lead a happier, more satisfying life.

ISBN: 1-55623-398-1 $19.95

Available at Fine Bookstores and Libraries Everywhere.

Please note: Prices quoted are in U.S. currency and are subject to change without notice.